50 No-Bake Dessert Recipes for Home

By: Kelly Johnson

Table of Contents

- No-Bake Chocolate Cheesecake
- Peanut Butter Chocolate Bars
- Strawberry Icebox Cake
- Lemon Icebox Pie
- Coconut Rum Balls
- Oreo Cheesecake Bites
- No-Bake Tiramisu
- Raspberry Coconut Squares
- Key Lime Pie Bars
- Chocolate Peanut Butter Pretzel Bars
- Mango Coconut Cheesecake
- No-Bake Cookie Dough Bars
- Chocolate Pudding Pie
- No-Bake Peanut Butter Pie
- No-Bake Banana Pudding
- Cherry Almond Energy Bites
- No-Bake Lemon Blueberry Cheesecake
- Chocolate Peanut Butter Cups
- Raspberry Almond Bars
- Salted Caramel Chocolate Tart
- No-Bake Strawberry Shortcake Bars
- Coconut Mango Rice Pudding
- Chocolate Avocado Mousse
- Peanut Butter Oatmeal Cookies
- No-Bake Pumpkin Pie
- Almond Joy Bars
- Strawberry Yogurt Pie
- No-Bake Nutella Cheesecake
- Lemon Coconut Truffles
- Vegan Chocolate Mousse
- No-Bake Caramel Apple Cheesecake Bars
- No-Bake Pistachio Cream Pie
- Raspberry Chia Pudding
- No-Bake S'mores Bars
- Chocolate Covered Strawberry Truffles

- No-Bake Berry Icebox Cake
- Mango Lime Sorbet
- No-Bake Cinnamon Rolls
- Blueberry Lemon Cheesecake Bars
- Pistachio Coconut Squares
- No-Bake Almond Butter Cookies
- Chocolate Cherry Icebox Cake
- Lemon Coconut Energy Bites
- No-Bake Cappuccino Pie
- Strawberry Pretzel Salad Bars
- Pineapple Coconut Tarts
- No-Bake Maple Walnut Cheesecake
- Vegan Chocolate Peanut Butter Pie
- Matcha Green Tea Coconut Bars
- No-Bake Red Velvet Cake

No-Bake Chocolate Cheesecake

Ingredients:

- For the Crust:
    - 1 1/2 cups chocolate cookie crumbs (from about 20 chocolate sandwich cookies)
    - 6 tablespoons unsalted butter, melted
- For the Filling:
    - 16 ounces (450g) cream cheese, softened
    - 1 cup powdered sugar
    - 1 teaspoon vanilla extract
    - 1/2 cup heavy cream
    - 10 ounces (280g) semi-sweet or dark chocolate, melted and cooled slightly
- For Topping (Optional):
    - Whipped cream
    - Chocolate shavings or sprinkles

Instructions:

1. Prepare the Crust:
    - In a mixing bowl, combine the chocolate cookie crumbs and melted butter. Stir until the crumbs are evenly coated.
    - Press the mixture into the bottom of a 9-inch (23cm) springform pan or pie dish. Use the back of a spoon or measuring cup to firmly pack the crust.
    - Place the crust in the refrigerator to chill while preparing the filling.
2. Make the Filling:
    - In a large mixing bowl, beat the softened cream cheese until smooth and creamy.
    - Add the powdered sugar and vanilla extract, and continue to beat until well combined and fluffy.
    - In a separate bowl, whip the heavy cream until stiff peaks form.
    - Gently fold the melted chocolate into the whipped cream until smooth and combined.
    - Gradually fold the chocolate whipped cream into the cream cheese mixture until fully incorporated.
3. Assemble the Cheesecake:
    - Pour the chocolate cheesecake filling over the prepared crust in the pan.
    - Smooth the top with a spatula.

- Cover the cheesecake with plastic wrap and refrigerate for at least 4 hours, preferably overnight, until set.
4. Serve:
    - Before serving, run a knife around the edge of the cheesecake to loosen it from the pan.
    - Remove the springform ring, if using.
    - Optionally, garnish the top with whipped cream and chocolate shavings or sprinkles.

Enjoy your delicious No-Bake Chocolate Cheesecake! This recipe yields a rich and creamy chocolate dessert that's perfect for any occasion.

Peanut Butter Chocolate Bars

Ingredients:

- For the Base:
    - 1 cup creamy peanut butter
    - 1/2 cup unsalted butter, melted
    - 2 cups graham cracker crumbs
    - 2 cups powdered sugar
- For the Chocolate Layer:
    - 2 cups semisweet or dark chocolate chips
    - 1/4 cup creamy peanut butter

Instructions:

1. Prepare the Base:
    - In a mixing bowl, combine the creamy peanut butter and melted butter until smooth.
    - Add the graham cracker crumbs and powdered sugar to the peanut butter mixture. Stir well until fully combined and the mixture resembles a thick dough.
2. Assemble the Bars:
    - Press the peanut butter mixture evenly into the bottom of a 9x13-inch (23x33cm) baking dish lined with parchment paper or foil. Use the back of a spoon or your hands to pack it down firmly.
3. Make the Chocolate Layer:
    - In a microwave-safe bowl or using a double boiler, melt the chocolate chips and remaining 1/4 cup of peanut butter together until smooth, stirring frequently.
4. Add the Chocolate Topping:
    - Pour the melted chocolate mixture over the peanut butter base in the baking dish, spreading it out evenly with a spatula.
5. Chill and Set:
    - Place the baking dish in the refrigerator for at least 2 hours, or until the chocolate layer is set.
6. Slice and Serve:
    - Once the bars are fully set, lift them out of the baking dish using the parchment paper or foil overhang.
    - Cut into bars or squares using a sharp knife.
    - Serve and enjoy!

These Peanut Butter Chocolate Bars are perfect for peanut butter and chocolate lovers alike. They're rich, creamy, and absolutely delicious! Store any leftovers in an airtight container in the refrigerator for up to a week.

Strawberry Icebox Cake

Ingredients:

- 1 pound fresh strawberries, washed and hulled
- 2 cups heavy cream
- 1/4 cup powdered sugar
- 1 teaspoon vanilla extract
- 1 (14.4 oz) box graham crackers

Optional Garnish:

- Additional fresh strawberries, sliced
- Mint leaves

Instructions:

1. Prepare the Whipped Cream:
    - In a large mixing bowl, whip the heavy cream, powdered sugar, and vanilla extract together until stiff peaks form. Set aside.
2. Slice the Strawberries:
    - Thinly slice the fresh strawberries and set aside.
3. Assemble the Cake:
    - Spread a thin layer of the whipped cream on the bottom of a 9x13-inch (23x33cm) baking dish or similar-sized dish.
    - Place a layer of graham crackers on top of the whipped cream, breaking them as needed to fit the dish and cover the bottom completely.
    - Spread a generous layer of whipped cream over the graham crackers, followed by a layer of sliced strawberries.
    - Repeat the layers: graham crackers, whipped cream, and strawberries, until you've used up all the ingredients, ending with a layer of whipped cream on top.
4. Chill the Cake:
    - Cover the dish with plastic wrap and refrigerate for at least 4 hours, or preferably overnight. Chilling allows the graham crackers to soften and absorb moisture, creating a cake-like texture.
5. Serve:
    - Before serving, garnish the top of the cake with additional sliced strawberries and mint leaves if desired.
    - Slice into squares and serve chilled.

This Strawberry Icebox Cake is a wonderful combination of creamy whipped cream, sweet strawberries, and soft graham crackers. It's easy to prepare and makes a stunning dessert for any occasion. Enjoy!

Lemon Icebox Pie

Ingredients:

- 1 (14 oz) can sweetened condensed milk
- 1/2 cup fresh lemon juice (about 3-4 lemons)
- 1 tablespoon lemon zest (from about 2 lemons)
- 2 cups heavy cream
- 1/4 cup powdered sugar
- 1 teaspoon vanilla extract
- 1 (9-inch) prepared graham cracker crust (store-bought or homemade)

Optional Garnish:

- Whipped cream
- Lemon slices
- Mint leaves

Instructions:

1. Prepare the Filling:
    - In a large mixing bowl, whisk together the sweetened condensed milk, fresh lemon juice, and lemon zest until smooth and well combined. The mixture will begin to thicken slightly due to the acidity of the lemon juice. Set aside.
2. Prepare the Whipped Cream:
    - In another mixing bowl, whip the heavy cream, powdered sugar, and vanilla extract together until stiff peaks form.
3. Combine the Filling and Whipped Cream:
    - Gently fold half of the whipped cream into the lemon mixture until fully incorporated and no streaks remain. Reserve the remaining whipped cream for topping.
4. Assemble the Pie:
    - Pour the lemon filling into the prepared graham cracker crust, spreading it out evenly with a spatula.
5. Chill the Pie:
    - Cover the pie with plastic wrap and refrigerate for at least 4 hours, or preferably overnight, to allow the filling to set.
6. Serve:
    - Before serving, top the pie with the reserved whipped cream.

- Optionally, garnish with lemon slices and mint leaves.

This Lemon Icebox Pie is creamy, zesty, and bursting with lemon flavor. It's a wonderful dessert to enjoy on a hot day or to serve at gatherings. Keep any leftovers refrigerated for up to a few days. Enjoy this delightful treat!

Coconut Rum Balls

Ingredients:

- 1 1/2 cups sweetened shredded coconut
- 1 cup crushed vanilla wafer cookies (about 30 cookies)
- 3/4 cup powdered sugar, plus extra for rolling
- 1/2 cup finely chopped pecans or walnuts
- 1/4 cup dark rum (or coconut rum for extra coconut flavor)
- 2 tablespoons light corn syrup or honey
- 1/2 teaspoon vanilla extract

Optional Coatings:

- Additional sweetened shredded coconut
- Cocoa powder
- Crushed nuts

Instructions:

1. Mix Dry Ingredients:
    - In a large bowl, combine the sweetened shredded coconut, crushed vanilla wafer cookies, powdered sugar, and chopped nuts. Stir until well mixed.
2. Add Wet Ingredients:
    - Pour in the dark rum, light corn syrup (or honey), and vanilla extract. Mix everything together until the mixture becomes moist and holds together. If it's too dry, add a bit more rum or corn syrup.
3. Shape into Balls:
    - Using your hands, scoop up about a tablespoon of the mixture and roll it into a ball between your palms. Place the formed balls on a baking sheet lined with parchment paper.
4. Coat the Balls:
    - Roll each ball in additional powdered sugar, sweetened shredded coconut, cocoa powder, or crushed nuts, depending on your preference. You can mix and match coatings for variety.
5. Chill and Set:
    - Place the coconut rum balls in the refrigerator to chill for at least 1 hour. This will help them firm up and hold their shape.
6. Serve and Enjoy:

- Once chilled and set, transfer the coconut rum balls to an airtight container and store them in the refrigerator until ready to serve.
- Enjoy these delicious Coconut Rum Balls as a sweet treat or dessert with a hint of tropical flavor!

These Coconut Rum Balls are perfect for parties, holidays, or simply as a delightful homemade treat. They have a lovely combination of coconut, rum, and sweetness, making them irresistible to coconut lovers and dessert enthusiasts alike. Adjust the rum and sweetness levels to suit your taste preferences. Enjoy!

Oreo Cheesecake Bites

Ingredients:

- 24 Oreo cookies (regular or Double Stuf)
- 8 ounces (225g) cream cheese, softened
- 1/4 cup powdered sugar
- 1 teaspoon vanilla extract
- 1 cup chocolate chips (semisweet or milk chocolate), melted
- Optional: Crushed Oreo cookies or sprinkles for garnish

Instructions:

1. Prepare the Oreo Crust:
    - Line a baking sheet or tray with parchment paper.
    - In a food processor or blender, crush 12 Oreo cookies into fine crumbs.
2. Make the Cheesecake Filling:
    - In a mixing bowl, combine the softened cream cheese, powdered sugar, and vanilla extract. Beat until smooth and creamy.
3. Mix the Cheesecake and Oreo Crumbs:
    - Add the crushed Oreo crumbs to the cream cheese mixture. Mix until well combined.
4. Form Cheesecake Balls:
    - Take about a tablespoon of the cheesecake mixture and roll it into a ball using your hands. Place it on the prepared baking sheet.
    - Repeat with the remaining cheesecake mixture to make about 24 cheesecake balls.
    - Freeze the cheesecake balls for about 30 minutes to firm up.
5. Dip Cheesecake Balls in Chocolate:
    - While the cheesecake balls are chilling, melt the chocolate chips in a microwave-safe bowl in 30-second intervals, stirring between each interval until smooth.
6. Coat the Cheesecake Balls:
    - Using a fork or toothpick, dip each chilled cheesecake ball into the melted chocolate, tapping off any excess chocolate.
    - Place the coated cheesecake ball back onto the parchment-lined baking sheet.
7. Garnish (Optional):
    - Immediately sprinkle crushed Oreo cookies or sprinkles on top of the chocolate-coated cheesecake balls before the chocolate sets.

8. Chill and Serve:
    - Refrigerate the Oreo Cheesecake Bites for at least 1 hour, or until the chocolate coating is set.
    - Serve chilled and enjoy these delightful Oreo Cheesecake Bites!

These Oreo Cheesecake Bites are perfect for parties, gatherings, or a sweet treat any time you're craving something deliciously creamy and chocolatey. Store any leftovers in an airtight container in the refrigerator. Enjoy!

No-Bake Tiramisu

Ingredients:

- 1 cup strong brewed coffee or espresso, cooled
- 2 tablespoons coffee liqueur (e.g., Kahlua), optional
- 8 oz (227g) mascarpone cheese, softened
- 1/2 cup powdered sugar
- 1 teaspoon vanilla extract
- 1 cup heavy cream
- 24-30 ladyfinger cookies (savoiardi)
- Unsweetened cocoa powder, for dusting

Instructions:

1. Prepare Coffee Mixture:
    - In a shallow dish, combine the cooled brewed coffee (or espresso) with the coffee liqueur (if using). Set aside.
2. Make Mascarpone Filling:
    - In a mixing bowl, beat the softened mascarpone cheese, powdered sugar, and vanilla extract until smooth and well combined.
3. Whip the Heavy Cream:
    - In a separate bowl, whip the heavy cream until stiff peaks form.
4. Combine Mascarpone and Whipped Cream:
    - Gently fold the whipped cream into the mascarpone mixture until smooth and creamy. Set aside.
5. Assemble the Tiramisu:
    - Quickly dip each ladyfinger cookie into the coffee mixture, ensuring they are moistened but not soaked through.
    - Arrange a layer of soaked ladyfingers in the bottom of a serving dish (such as a square baking dish or trifle dish).
6. Add Mascarpone Cream Layer:
    - Spread half of the mascarpone cream mixture evenly over the layer of soaked ladyfingers.
7. Repeat Layers:
    - Create another layer of soaked ladyfingers on top of the mascarpone cream layer.
    - Spread the remaining mascarpone cream mixture evenly over the second layer of ladyfingers.
8. Chill and Set:

- Cover the dish with plastic wrap and refrigerate for at least 4 hours, preferably overnight, to allow the tiramisu to set and flavors to meld together.

9. Dust with Cocoa Powder:
   - Before serving, dust the top of the tiramisu with unsweetened cocoa powder using a fine-mesh sieve.

10. Serve and Enjoy:
    - Slice and serve the delicious no-bake tiramisu chilled. It's a perfect dessert for gatherings and celebrations!

This no-bake tiramisu recipe is simple yet elegant, offering all the flavors of the traditional dessert without the need for baking. Enjoy the creamy texture, coffee-infused ladyfingers, and rich mascarpone filling with every bite. Buon appetito!

Raspberry Coconut Squares

Ingredients:

For the Base:

- 1 1/2 cups graham cracker crumbs
- 1/2 cup unsalted butter, melted

For the Raspberry Layer:

- 2 cups fresh raspberries (or frozen, thawed)
- 1/4 cup granulated sugar
- 1 tablespoon cornstarch

For the Coconut Layer:

- 1 (14 oz) can sweetened condensed milk
- 2 cups shredded coconut (sweetened)

For Garnish (optional):

- Fresh raspberries
- Shredded coconut

Instructions:

1. Prepare the Base:
   - In a mixing bowl, combine the graham cracker crumbs and melted butter. Stir until the crumbs are evenly coated.
   - Press the mixture into the bottom of an 8x8-inch (20x20cm) baking dish lined with parchment paper. Use the back of a spoon or measuring cup to firmly pack the crust.
   - Place the crust in the refrigerator to chill while preparing the filling.
2. Make the Raspberry Layer:
   - In a saucepan, combine the raspberries, sugar, and cornstarch. Cook over medium heat, stirring frequently, until the raspberries break down and the mixture thickens (about 5-7 minutes).
   - Remove from heat and let it cool slightly.
3. Prepare the Coconut Layer:
   - In a mixing bowl, combine the sweetened condensed milk and shredded coconut. Mix until well combined.

4. **Assemble the Squares:**
   - Spread the raspberry mixture evenly over the chilled graham cracker crust.
   - Spoon the coconut mixture over the raspberry layer, spreading it out with a spatula to cover evenly.
5. **Chill and Set:**
   - Refrigerate the raspberry coconut squares for at least 2 hours, or until firm and set.
6. **Slice and Garnish (optional):**
   - Once set, lift the squares out of the baking dish using the parchment paper overhang.
   - Cut into squares using a sharp knife.
   - Garnish each square with fresh raspberries and a sprinkle of shredded coconut, if desired.
7. **Serve and Enjoy:**
   - Serve these delicious raspberry coconut squares chilled as a delightful dessert or sweet treat.

These Raspberry Coconut Squares are perfect for parties, potlucks, or any occasion. They're bursting with fruity and coconut flavors, and the no-bake preparation makes them quick and easy to whip up. Enjoy this delightful dessert!

Key Lime Pie Bars

Ingredients:

For the Crust:

- 1 1/2 cups graham cracker crumbs
- 1/3 cup granulated sugar
- 1/2 cup unsalted butter, melted

For the Filling:

- 1 (14 oz) can sweetened condensed milk
- 3/4 cup key lime juice (freshly squeezed or bottled)
- Zest of 2 limes (optional)
- 3 large egg yolks

For Garnish (optional):

- Whipped cream
- Lime slices
- Lime zest

Instructions:

1. Preheat the Oven:
    - Preheat your oven to 350°F (175°C). Line an 8x8-inch (20x20cm) baking dish with parchment paper, leaving an overhang for easy removal.
2. Make the Crust:
    - In a mixing bowl, combine the graham cracker crumbs, granulated sugar, and melted butter. Mix until well combined and the mixture resembles wet sand.
    - Press the crust mixture evenly into the bottom of the prepared baking dish.
3. Bake the Crust:
    - Bake the crust in the preheated oven for 8-10 minutes, or until lightly golden and set. Remove from the oven and set aside to cool slightly.
4. Prepare the Filling:
    - In another mixing bowl, whisk together the sweetened condensed milk, key lime juice, lime zest (if using), and egg yolks until smooth and well combined.
5. Assemble and Bake:
    - Pour the filling mixture over the baked crust, spreading it out evenly.

6. Bake the Bars:
   - Return the baking dish to the oven and bake for 15-18 minutes, or until the filling is set and the edges are just beginning to turn golden.
7. Chill and Set:
   - Remove the baking dish from the oven and let the key lime pie bars cool completely at room temperature.
   - Once cooled, refrigerate the bars for at least 2 hours, or until fully chilled and set.
8. Slice and Garnish:
   - Lift the key lime pie bars out of the baking dish using the parchment paper overhang.
   - Cut into squares or bars using a sharp knife.
   - Optionally, garnish each bar with a dollop of whipped cream, a slice of lime, and a sprinkle of lime zest.
9. Serve and Enjoy:
   - Serve these delicious key lime pie bars chilled as a refreshing dessert. They're tangy, creamy, and perfect for lime lovers!

These Key Lime Pie Bars are a wonderful treat for any occasion, and they can be made ahead of time for easy serving. Enjoy the zesty and creamy flavors of key lime pie in a convenient bar form!

Chocolate Peanut Butter Pretzel Bars

Ingredients:

For the Base:

- 2 cups pretzel rods, crushed into small pieces
- 1 cup creamy peanut butter
- 1/2 cup honey or maple syrup

For the Chocolate Layer:

- 1 1/2 cups semi-sweet chocolate chips
- 1/2 cup creamy peanut butter

Instructions:

1. Prepare the Base:
    - Line an 8x8-inch (20x20cm) baking dish with parchment paper.
    - In a mixing bowl, combine the crushed pretzel pieces, creamy peanut butter, and honey (or maple syrup). Stir until well combined and the pretzel pieces are coated evenly.
2. Press into Pan:
    - Press the pretzel mixture firmly and evenly into the bottom of the prepared baking dish using the back of a spoon or spatula. Ensure it forms a compact and even layer.
3. Make the Chocolate Layer:
    - In a microwave-safe bowl or using a double boiler, melt the chocolate chips and creamy peanut butter together until smooth, stirring frequently.
4. Pour Over Pretzel Base:
    - Pour the melted chocolate-peanut butter mixture over the pretzel base in the baking dish, spreading it out evenly with a spatula.
5. Chill and Set:
    - Place the baking dish in the refrigerator for at least 1-2 hours, or until the chocolate layer is completely set and firm.
6. Slice and Serve:
    - Once set, lift the bars out of the baking dish using the parchment paper overhang.
    - Cut into bars or squares using a sharp knife.
7. Enjoy:
    - Serve these delicious Chocolate Peanut Butter Pretzel Bars chilled. They are perfect for snacking or as a sweet treat.

Optional Variations:

- Additions: Feel free to add chopped nuts (like peanuts or almonds) or mini chocolate chips to the pretzel base for extra texture.
- Toppings: Sprinkle some sea salt over the chocolate layer before it sets for a salted chocolate flavor.

These Chocolate Peanut Butter Pretzel Bars are a crowd-pleaser, combining the irresistible combination of chocolate, peanut butter, and crunchy pretzels. Enjoy making and sharing these delightful bars!

Mango Coconut Cheesecake

Ingredients:

For the Crust:

- 1 1/2 cups graham cracker crumbs
- 1/4 cup granulated sugar
- 1/2 cup unsalted butter, melted

For the Cheesecake Filling:

- 16 oz (450g) cream cheese, softened
- 1/2 cup granulated sugar
- 1 teaspoon vanilla extract
- 1 cup mango puree (from fresh or canned mango)
- 1 cup shredded coconut (sweetened or unsweetened)
- 1 cup heavy cream

For Garnish (optional):

- Sliced fresh mango
- Toasted coconut flakes

Instructions:

1. Prepare the Crust:
   - In a mixing bowl, combine the graham cracker crumbs, granulated sugar, and melted butter. Stir until well combined.
   - Press the mixture firmly into the bottom of a 9-inch (23cm) springform pan or pie dish. Use the back of a spoon or measuring cup to pack it down evenly.
   - Place the crust in the refrigerator to chill while preparing the filling.
2. Make the Cheesecake Filling:
   - In a large mixing bowl, beat the softened cream cheese, sugar, and vanilla extract until smooth and creamy.
   - Add the mango puree and shredded coconut to the cream cheese mixture. Mix until well combined.
3. Whip the Heavy Cream:
   - In a separate bowl, whip the heavy cream until stiff peaks form.
4. Combine and Assemble:
   - Gently fold the whipped cream into the mango-coconut cream cheese mixture until smooth and fully combined.
   - Pour the filling over the prepared graham cracker crust, spreading it out evenly with a spatula.
5. Chill and Set:

- Cover the cheesecake with plastic wrap and refrigerate for at least 4 hours, preferably overnight, to allow it to set and firm up.
6. Garnish and Serve:
    - Before serving, garnish the mango coconut cheesecake with sliced fresh mango and toasted coconut flakes, if desired.
7. Slice and Enjoy:
    - Use a sharp knife to slice the cheesecake into wedges.
    - Serve chilled and enjoy the tropical flavors of mango and coconut in this delightful no-bake cheesecake!

This Mango Coconut Cheesecake is creamy, fruity, and perfect for summer gatherings or special occasions. It's a wonderful dessert that will impress your guests and satisfy your sweet cravings. Enjoy!

No-Bake Cookie Dough Bars

Ingredients:

For the Cookie Dough Layer:

- 1/2 cup unsalted butter, softened
- 3/4 cup light brown sugar, packed
- 1 teaspoon vanilla extract
- 1 1/2 cups all-purpose flour
- 1/4 teaspoon salt
- 1 cup mini chocolate chips
- 1/4 cup milk (add more as needed for desired consistency)

For the Chocolate Topping:

- 1 1/2 cups semi-sweet or milk chocolate chips
- 2 tablespoons unsalted butter

Instructions:

1. Prepare the Cookie Dough Layer:
   - In a mixing bowl, cream together the softened butter and brown sugar until light and fluffy.
   - Add the vanilla extract and mix until combined.
   - Gradually add the flour and salt to the mixture, mixing until well incorporated.
   - Stir in the mini chocolate chips.
   - Add the milk gradually, mixing until the dough reaches a smooth and slightly firm consistency that holds together when pressed. You may not need to use all of the milk.
2. Press into Pan:
   - Line an 8x8-inch (20x20cm) baking dish with parchment paper, leaving an overhang on the sides for easy removal.
   - Press the cookie dough mixture evenly into the bottom of the prepared baking dish. Use a spatula or the back of a spoon to smooth out the surface.
3. Make the Chocolate Topping:
   - In a microwave-safe bowl or using a double boiler, melt the chocolate chips and unsalted butter together until smooth and glossy, stirring frequently.

4. Pour Over Cookie Dough Layer:
   - Pour the melted chocolate mixture over the cookie dough layer, spreading it out evenly with a spatula.
5. Chill and Set:
   - Place the baking dish in the refrigerator for at least 1-2 hours, or until the chocolate topping is set and firm.
6. Slice and Serve:
   - Once set, lift the bars out of the baking dish using the parchment paper overhang.
   - Use a sharp knife to cut the bars into squares or rectangles.
7. Enjoy:
   - Serve these delicious No-Bake Cookie Dough Bars chilled as a sweet and indulgent treat!

These Cookie Dough Bars are perfect for satisfying your cookie dough cravings without any baking required. Store any leftovers in an airtight container in the refrigerator for up to a week. Enjoy these delightful bars as a snack or dessert!

Chocolate Pudding Pie

Ingredients:

For the Chocolate Cookie Crust:

- 1 1/2 cups chocolate cookie crumbs (from about 20 chocolate sandwich cookies)
- 6 tablespoons unsalted butter, melted

For the Chocolate Pudding Filling:

- 1/2 cup granulated sugar
- 1/4 cup cornstarch
- 1/4 teaspoon salt
- 3 cups whole milk
- 6 ounces semi-sweet chocolate, finely chopped (or use chocolate chips)
- 2 tablespoons unsalted butter
- 1 teaspoon vanilla extract

For Garnish (optional):

- Whipped cream
- Chocolate shavings or sprinkles

Instructions:

1. Make the Chocolate Cookie Crust:
    - Preheat your oven to 350°F (175°C).
    - In a bowl, combine the chocolate cookie crumbs and melted butter. Mix until well combined.
    - Press the mixture into the bottom and up the sides of a 9-inch (23cm) pie dish to form the crust.
    - Bake the crust in the preheated oven for 8-10 minutes. Remove from the oven and let it cool completely.
2. Prepare the Chocolate Pudding Filling:
    - In a medium saucepan, whisk together the granulated sugar, cornstarch, and salt.
    - Gradually whisk in the whole milk until smooth and no lumps remain.
    - Place the saucepan over medium heat and cook, stirring constantly, until the mixture thickens and starts to boil (about 5-7 minutes).
3. Add Chocolate and Butter:

- Remove the saucepan from the heat and immediately add the finely chopped semi-sweet chocolate, unsalted butter, and vanilla extract.
- Stir until the chocolate and butter are melted and the mixture is smooth and creamy.
4. Assemble the Pie:
    - Pour the chocolate pudding filling into the cooled chocolate cookie crust, smoothing out the top with a spatula.
5. Chill the Pie:
    - Cover the pie with plastic wrap, ensuring the wrap touches the surface of the pudding to prevent a skin from forming.
    - Refrigerate the chocolate pudding pie for at least 4 hours, or until the filling is fully set.
6. Garnish and Serve:
    - Before serving, garnish the chocolate pudding pie with whipped cream and chocolate shavings or sprinkles, if desired.
7. Slice and Enjoy:
    - Use a sharp knife to cut the chilled chocolate pudding pie into slices.
    - Serve and enjoy this creamy and decadent dessert!

This chocolate pudding pie is perfect for chocolate lovers and makes a wonderful treat for any occasion. It's smooth, silky, and sure to satisfy your sweet cravings. Store any leftovers in the refrigerator and enjoy within a few days. Enjoy this delightful chocolatey dessert!

No-Bake Peanut Butter Pie

Ingredients:

For the Crust:

- 1 1/2 cups graham cracker crumbs
- 1/4 cup granulated sugar
- 6 tablespoons unsalted butter, melted

For the Filling:

- 1 cup creamy peanut butter
- 8 oz (225g) cream cheese, softened
- 1 cup powdered sugar
- 1 teaspoon vanilla extract
- 1 cup heavy cream, chilled

For Garnish (optional):

- Whipped cream
- Chopped peanuts
- Chocolate sauce

Instructions:

1. Make the Crust:
   - In a mixing bowl, combine the graham cracker crumbs, granulated sugar, and melted butter. Stir until well combined and the mixture resembles wet sand.
   - Press the mixture firmly and evenly into the bottom and up the sides of a 9-inch (23cm) pie dish. Use the back of a spoon or measuring cup to pack the crust.
   - Place the crust in the refrigerator to chill while preparing the filling.
2. Prepare the Filling:
   - In a large mixing bowl, beat the creamy peanut butter and softened cream cheese until smooth and well combined.
   - Add the powdered sugar and vanilla extract, and continue to beat until creamy and smooth.
3. Whip the Heavy Cream:
   - In a separate bowl, whip the chilled heavy cream until stiff peaks form.
4. Combine and Assemble:

- Gently fold the whipped cream into the peanut butter mixture until smooth and well incorporated.
5. Fill the Pie Crust:
    - Spoon the peanut butter filling into the chilled crust, spreading it out evenly with a spatula.
6. Chill and Set:
    - Cover the pie with plastic wrap and refrigerate for at least 4 hours, or until the filling is firm and set.
7. Garnish and Serve:
    - Before serving, garnish the peanut butter pie with whipped cream, chopped peanuts, and a drizzle of chocolate sauce, if desired.
8. Slice and Enjoy:
    - Use a sharp knife to slice the chilled peanut butter pie into wedges.
    - Serve and enjoy this creamy and indulgent no-bake dessert!

This No-Bake Peanut Butter Pie is creamy, rich, and packed with peanut butter flavor. It's a crowd-pleaser and a perfect treat for any occasion. Store any leftovers in the refrigerator and enjoy within a few days. Dig in and savor every bite of this delicious peanut butter pie!

No-Bake Banana Pudding

Ingredients:

- 1 box (3.4 oz) instant vanilla pudding mix
- 2 cups cold milk
- 1 can (14 oz) sweetened condensed milk
- 1 teaspoon vanilla extract
- 2 cups heavy cream, chilled
- 1 box (11 oz) vanilla wafers
- 4-5 ripe bananas, sliced
- Whipped cream for garnish (optional)

Instructions:

1. Prepare the Pudding Mixture:
    - In a large mixing bowl, whisk together the instant vanilla pudding mix and cold milk until smooth and slightly thickened.
    - Add the sweetened condensed milk and vanilla extract to the pudding mixture. Stir until well combined and smooth.
2. Whip the Heavy Cream:
    - In another bowl, whip the chilled heavy cream using a hand mixer or stand mixer until stiff peaks form.
3. Combine Pudding and Whipped Cream:
    - Gently fold the whipped cream into the pudding mixture until well incorporated and creamy.
4. Assemble the Banana Pudding:
    - In a serving dish or trifle bowl, start layering the ingredients. Begin with a layer of vanilla wafers on the bottom of the dish.
    - Top the wafers with a layer of sliced bananas.
    - Spoon a layer of the pudding mixture over the bananas, spreading it out evenly.
    - Continue layering with vanilla wafers, bananas, and pudding until all ingredients are used, finishing with a layer of pudding on top.
5. Chill and Set:
    - Cover the banana pudding with plastic wrap and refrigerate for at least 4 hours, or preferably overnight, to allow the flavors to meld and the pudding to set.
6. Serve and Garnish:

- Before serving, garnish the chilled banana pudding with additional vanilla wafers and sliced bananas on top.
- Optionally, add a dollop of whipped cream for extra indulgence.

7. **Enjoy:**
   - Scoop the chilled no-bake banana pudding into bowls or dessert cups and serve cold.

This no-bake banana pudding is creamy, flavorful, and perfect for potlucks, parties, or a simple family dessert. The combination of bananas, vanilla wafers, and creamy pudding is a classic and irresistible treat. Enjoy every spoonful of this delicious dessert!

Cherry Almond Energy Bites

Ingredients:

- 1 cup rolled oats
- 1/2 cup dried cherries, chopped
- 1/2 cup almond butter (or any nut butter of your choice)
- 1/4 cup honey or maple syrup
- 1/4 cup almond meal or ground almonds
- 1/4 cup unsweetened shredded coconut
- 1 teaspoon almond extract (optional)
- Pinch of salt

Optional Additions:

- 1/4 cup mini chocolate chips
- Chopped almonds or other nuts for extra crunch

Instructions:

1. Combine Ingredients:
    - In a large mixing bowl, combine the rolled oats, chopped dried cherries, almond butter, honey or maple syrup, almond meal, shredded coconut, almond extract (if using), and a pinch of salt.
    - Mix all the ingredients together until well combined. The mixture should be sticky and hold together when pressed.
2. Form into Bites:
    - Take small portions of the mixture and roll them into bite-sized balls using your hands. If the mixture is too sticky, you can wet your hands slightly with water.
    - Continue until all the mixture is used up, and you have formed several energy bites.
3. Optional Coating:
    - Roll the energy bites in additional shredded coconut, chopped nuts, or mini chocolate chips for an extra layer of flavor and texture.
4. Chill and Set:
    - Place the energy bites on a baking sheet lined with parchment paper and refrigerate for at least 30 minutes to allow them to firm up.
5. Store and Enjoy:

- Once chilled and set, transfer the cherry almond energy bites to an airtight container.
- Keep them refrigerated for up to one week. Enjoy as a quick snack or energy boost throughout the day!

These Cherry Almond Energy Bites are nutritious, satisfying, and make a great on-the-go snack. They're loaded with fiber, protein, and healthy fats from the almonds and oats, making them a perfect choice for a quick and tasty treat. Customize the recipe by adding your favorite mix-ins and enjoy these delicious bites whenever you need a pick-me-up!

No-Bake Lemon Blueberry Cheesecake

Ingredients:

For the Crust:

- 1 1/2 cups graham cracker crumbs
- 1/4 cup granulated sugar
- 6 tablespoons unsalted butter, melted

For the Cheesecake Filling:

- 16 oz (450g) cream cheese, softened
- 1 cup powdered sugar
- Zest of 1 lemon
- 2 tablespoons fresh lemon juice
- 1 teaspoon vanilla extract
- 1 cup fresh blueberries

For the Topping:

- 1 cup fresh blueberries
- 1/4 cup granulated sugar
- 2 tablespoons water
- 1 tablespoon cornstarch
- Zest of 1 lemon
- Additional fresh blueberries and lemon zest for garnish

Instructions:

1. Prepare the Crust:
   - In a mixing bowl, combine the graham cracker crumbs, granulated sugar, and melted butter. Stir until the crumbs are evenly coated.
   - Press the mixture firmly and evenly into the bottom of a 9-inch (23cm) springform pan. Use the back of a spoon or measuring cup to pack the crust.
   - Place the crust in the refrigerator to chill while preparing the filling.
2. Make the Blueberry Topping:
   - In a saucepan, combine 1 cup of fresh blueberries, granulated sugar, water, cornstarch, and lemon zest.
   - Cook over medium heat, stirring frequently, until the mixture thickens and the blueberries burst (about 5-7 minutes).
   - Remove from heat and let it cool completely.
3. Prepare the Cheesecake Filling:
   - In a large mixing bowl, beat the softened cream cheese and powdered sugar until smooth and creamy.

- Add the lemon zest, fresh lemon juice, and vanilla extract to the cream cheese mixture. Mix until well combined and smooth.
4. Assemble the Cheesecake:
   - Gently fold 1 cup of fresh blueberries into the prepared cheesecake filling.
   - Spread the cheesecake filling evenly over the chilled graham cracker crust.
5. Add the Blueberry Topping:
   - Spoon the cooled blueberry topping over the cheesecake filling, spreading it out evenly.
6. Chill and Set:
   - Cover the cheesecake with plastic wrap and refrigerate for at least 4 hours, preferably overnight, to allow it to set and firm up.
7. Garnish and Serve:
   - Before serving, garnish the lemon blueberry cheesecake with additional fresh blueberries and lemon zest.
8. Slice and Enjoy:
   - Use a sharp knife to slice the chilled cheesecake into wedges.
   - Serve and enjoy this delightful no-bake dessert with a perfect balance of lemon and blueberry flavors!

This No-Bake Lemon Blueberry Cheesecake is creamy, fruity, and bursting with flavor. It's a wonderful dessert for summer gatherings or any special occasion. Store any leftovers in the refrigerator. Enjoy every bite of this delicious cheesecake!

Chocolate Peanut Butter Cups

Ingredients:

- 12 oz (340g) semi-sweet or milk chocolate chips
- 1 cup creamy peanut butter
- 1/4 cup powdered sugar (optional, for sweeter filling)
- 2 tablespoons unsalted butter, softened
- 1 teaspoon vanilla extract
- Pinch of salt

Instructions:

1. Prepare the Chocolate Coating:
    - Line a standard muffin tin with 12 paper or silicone cupcake liners.
    - In a microwave-safe bowl or using a double boiler, melt the chocolate chips until smooth and completely melted. Stir occasionally to ensure even melting.
2. Prepare the Peanut Butter Filling:
    - In a separate mixing bowl, combine the creamy peanut butter, powdered sugar (if using), softened butter, vanilla extract, and a pinch of salt. Mix until smooth and well combined. Adjust sweetness to taste by adding more powdered sugar if desired.
3. Assemble the Peanut Butter Cups:
    - Spoon a small amount of melted chocolate into the bottom of each cupcake liner, spreading it to cover the bottom and slightly up the sides.
    - Place the muffin tin in the refrigerator for about 10 minutes to allow the chocolate to set.
4. Add the Peanut Butter Filling:
    - Once the chocolate base has set, spoon a generous amount of peanut butter filling into each cup, pressing it down gently to flatten and spread evenly.
5. Top with Remaining Chocolate:
    - Pour the remaining melted chocolate over the peanut butter filling in each cup, covering it completely and smoothing out the top with a spoon.
6. Chill and Set:
    - Return the muffin tin to the refrigerator and chill for at least 1 hour, or until the chocolate is firm and set.
7. Serve and Enjoy:

- Once fully set, remove the chocolate peanut butter cups from the muffin tin and peel off the paper liners.
- Serve and enjoy these homemade chocolate peanut butter cups as a delightful treat!

8. Storage:
   - Store any leftover chocolate peanut butter cups in an airtight container in the refrigerator for up to one week. Bring to room temperature before serving for best texture.

These homemade Chocolate Peanut Butter Cups are sure to impress and are perfect for sharing with family and friends. They make a wonderful gift and can be customized with different types of chocolate or peanut butter. Enjoy these delicious treats anytime you're craving a combination of chocolate and peanut butter goodness!

Raspberry Almond Bars

Ingredients:

For the Crust:

- 1 cup all-purpose flour
- 1/2 cup granulated sugar
- 1/4 teaspoon salt
- 1/2 cup unsalted butter, cold and cut into small pieces

For the Raspberry Filling:

- 12 oz (about 2 cups) fresh raspberries
- 1/4 cup granulated sugar
- 2 tablespoons cornstarch
- 1 tablespoon lemon juice

For the Almond Topping:

- 1 cup sliced almonds
- 1/4 cup unsalted butter, melted
- 1/3 cup brown sugar
- 1/4 cup all-purpose flour
- 1/4 teaspoon almond extract

Instructions:

1. Preheat the Oven:
    - Preheat your oven to 350°F (175°C). Grease or line a 9x9-inch (23x23cm) baking pan with parchment paper.
2. Make the Crust:
    - In a mixing bowl, combine the flour, granulated sugar, and salt.
    - Cut in the cold butter using a pastry cutter or fork until the mixture resembles coarse crumbs.
    - Press the mixture evenly into the bottom of the prepared baking pan.
    - Bake the crust in the preheated oven for 15-18 minutes, or until lightly golden brown. Remove from the oven and let it cool slightly.
3. Prepare the Raspberry Filling:
    - In a saucepan, combine the fresh raspberries, granulated sugar, cornstarch, and lemon juice.

- Cook over medium heat, stirring frequently, until the mixture thickens and the raspberries break down (about 5-7 minutes).
- Remove from heat and let it cool slightly.
4. Make the Almond Topping:
    - In a mixing bowl, combine the sliced almonds, melted butter, brown sugar, flour, and almond extract. Mix until well combined.
5. Assemble and Bake:
    - Spread the raspberry filling evenly over the baked crust.
    - Sprinkle the almond topping over the raspberry filling, covering it completely.
6. Bake Again:
    - Return the pan to the oven and bake for an additional 25-30 minutes, or until the almond topping is golden brown and crispy.
7. Cool and Serve:
    - Allow the raspberry almond bars to cool completely in the pan before slicing into bars.
8. Serve and Enjoy:
    - Once cooled, cut the bars into squares and serve. These bars are delicious on their own or with a scoop of vanilla ice cream.

These Raspberry Almond Bars are a delightful combination of flavors and textures, making them a perfect dessert for gatherings or everyday treats. Store any leftovers in an airtight container at room temperature for a few days. Enjoy the sweet and nutty goodness of these raspberry almond bars!

Salted Caramel Chocolate Tart

Ingredients:

For the Chocolate Tart Shell:

- 1 1/2 cups chocolate cookie crumbs (from about 20 chocolate sandwich cookies)
- 6 tablespoons unsalted butter, melted

For the Salted Caramel Filling:

- 1 cup granulated sugar
- 6 tablespoons unsalted butter, cubed
- 1/2 cup heavy cream
- 1 teaspoon vanilla extract
- 1/2 teaspoon sea salt (plus more for sprinkling)

For the Chocolate Ganache:

- 1 cup semi-sweet or dark chocolate chips
- 1/2 cup heavy cream

Instructions:

1. Prepare the Chocolate Tart Shell:
    - Preheat your oven to 350°F (175°C).
    - In a bowl, combine the chocolate cookie crumbs and melted butter. Mix until well combined.
    - Press the mixture evenly into the bottom and up the sides of a 9-inch (23cm) tart pan with a removable bottom.
    - Bake the tart shell in the preheated oven for 10 minutes. Remove from the oven and let it cool completely.
2. Make the Salted Caramel Filling:
    - In a heavy-bottomed saucepan, heat the granulated sugar over medium heat, stirring constantly with a wooden spoon or heat-resistant spatula.
    - Continue stirring until the sugar melts and turns into a golden amber color (be careful not to burn).
    - Carefully add the cubed butter to the melted sugar, stirring constantly until the butter is completely melted and combined.
    - Slowly pour in the heavy cream while stirring continuously. Be cautious as the mixture will bubble up.
    - Cook the caramel mixture for another 1-2 minutes, then remove from heat.
    - Stir in the vanilla extract and sea salt. Let the caramel cool slightly.
3. Assemble the Tart:
    - Pour the warm salted caramel filling into the cooled chocolate tart shell, spreading it out evenly.

- Place the tart in the refrigerator to chill and set for about 30 minutes.
4. Make the Chocolate Ganache:
    - In a microwave-safe bowl or heatproof bowl set over a pot of simmering water (double boiler), combine the chocolate chips and heavy cream.
    - Stir until the chocolate is completely melted and smooth.
5. Pour the Ganache Over the Tart:
    - Remove the chilled tart from the refrigerator and pour the chocolate ganache over the salted caramel layer, spreading it out evenly with a spatula.
6. Chill and Set:
    - Return the tart to the refrigerator and chill for at least 2 hours, or until the chocolate ganache is set.
7. Serve and Enjoy:
    - Before serving, sprinkle a bit of sea salt over the top of the tart for garnish.
    - Slice the tart into wedges and serve chilled. Enjoy the rich and decadent flavors of this salted caramel chocolate tart!

This Salted Caramel Chocolate Tart is a show-stopping dessert that's perfect for special occasions or any time you're craving a luxurious treat. The combination of chocolate, caramel, and sea salt is simply irresistible. Store any leftovers in the refrigerator for a few days. Enjoy every delightful bite of this indulgent tart!

No-Bake Strawberry Shortcake Bars

Ingredients:

For the Crust:

- 2 cups crushed shortbread cookies (about 10-12 cookies)
- 1/2 cup unsalted butter, melted

For the Strawberry Filling:

- 2 cups fresh strawberries, hulled and chopped
- 1/4 cup granulated sugar
- 1 tablespoon cornstarch
- 1 tablespoon water

For the Cream Cheese Layer:

- 8 oz (225g) cream cheese, softened
- 1/2 cup powdered sugar
- 1 teaspoon vanilla extract
- 1 cup heavy cream, chilled

For Garnish:

- Fresh strawberries, sliced
- Whipped cream (optional)

Instructions:

1. Prepare the Crust:
    - In a mixing bowl, combine the crushed shortbread cookies and melted butter. Mix until the crumbs are evenly coated.
    - Press the mixture firmly and evenly into the bottom of a 9x9-inch (23x23cm) square baking dish lined with parchment paper.
    - Place the crust in the refrigerator to chill while preparing the filling.
2. Make the Strawberry Filling:
    - In a saucepan, combine the chopped strawberries, granulated sugar, cornstarch, and water.
    - Cook over medium heat, stirring frequently, until the strawberries break down and the mixture thickens (about 5-7 minutes).
    - Remove from heat and let the strawberry filling cool completely.

3. Prepare the Cream Cheese Layer:
   - In a large mixing bowl, beat the softened cream cheese, powdered sugar, and vanilla extract until smooth and creamy.
   - In another bowl, whip the chilled heavy cream until stiff peaks form.
   - Gently fold the whipped cream into the cream cheese mixture until well combined.
4. Assemble the Bars:
   - Spread the cream cheese mixture evenly over the chilled shortbread crust in the baking dish.
   - Spoon the cooled strawberry filling over the cream cheese layer, spreading it out evenly.
5. Chill and Set:
   - Cover the baking dish with plastic wrap and refrigerate for at least 4 hours, preferably overnight, to allow the bars to set.
6. Garnish and Serve:
   - Before serving, garnish the bars with sliced fresh strawberries and a dollop of whipped cream, if desired.
7. Slice and Enjoy:
   - Use a sharp knife to cut the chilled strawberry shortcake bars into squares.
   - Serve and enjoy these delicious no-bake bars as a refreshing and delightful dessert!

These No-Bake Strawberry Shortcake Bars are perfect for summer gatherings, picnics, or anytime you want to enjoy the flavors of strawberry shortcake without turning on the oven. Store any leftovers in the refrigerator and enjoy within a few days. Each bite is creamy, fruity, and simply irresistible!

Coconut Mango Rice Pudding

Ingredients:

- 1 cup jasmine rice (or any medium-grain rice)
- 1 can (13.5 oz) full-fat coconut milk
- 2 cups water
- 1/4 cup granulated sugar (adjust to taste)
- Pinch of salt
- 1 ripe mango, peeled and diced
- 1/2 cup sweetened shredded coconut (optional)
- 1 teaspoon vanilla extract

Instructions:

1. Cook the Rice:
    - Rinse the jasmine rice under cold water until the water runs clear.
    - In a medium saucepan, combine the rinsed rice, coconut milk, water, sugar, and a pinch of salt.
    - Bring the mixture to a boil over medium-high heat, then reduce the heat to low and cover the saucepan with a lid.
    - Simmer the rice for about 15-20 minutes, stirring occasionally, until the rice is tender and has absorbed most of the liquid.
2. Add Mango and Coconut:
    - Once the rice is cooked and creamy, stir in the diced mango, sweetened shredded coconut (if using), and vanilla extract.
    - Continue cooking for another 2-3 minutes, allowing the flavors to meld together.
3. Serve Warm or Chilled:
    - Remove the saucepan from the heat.
    - Serve the coconut mango rice pudding warm or chilled, depending on your preference.
    - If serving chilled, transfer the rice pudding to a bowl or individual serving dishes and refrigerate until cold.
4. Garnish and Enjoy:
    - Optionally, garnish the coconut mango rice pudding with additional diced mangoes, shredded coconut, or a sprinkle of cinnamon before serving.
5. Store Leftovers:
    - Store any leftover coconut mango rice pudding in an airtight container in the refrigerator for up to 3-4 days.

- Enjoy this delicious dessert as a refreshing treat on its own or as a delightful ending to a tropical-inspired meal!

This Coconut Mango Rice Pudding is creamy, aromatic, and bursting with tropical flavors. It's a comforting dessert that's perfect for enjoying year-round, whether you serve it warm during cooler months or chilled during hot summer days. Treat yourself to this delightful treat and savor the wonderful combination of coconut, mango, and rice in every spoonful!

Chocolate Avocado Mousse

Ingredients:

- 2 ripe avocados
- 1/3 cup cocoa powder (unsweetened)
- 1/4 cup maple syrup or honey (adjust to taste)
- 1 teaspoon vanilla extract
- Pinch of salt
- Optional toppings: sliced strawberries, raspberries, chopped nuts, or shaved chocolate

Instructions:

1. Prepare the Avocados:
   - Cut the avocados in half, remove the pits, and scoop the flesh into a blender or food processor.
2. Blend the Ingredients:
   - Add the cocoa powder, maple syrup or honey, vanilla extract, and a pinch of salt to the blender or food processor with the avocados.
   - Blend until smooth and creamy, scraping down the sides of the blender or food processor as needed to ensure all ingredients are well combined.
3. Adjust Sweetness:
   - Taste the chocolate avocado mixture and adjust the sweetness by adding more maple syrup or honey if desired.
4. Chill (Optional):
   - For a firmer texture, transfer the chocolate avocado mousse to a bowl or individual serving dishes and chill in the refrigerator for about 30 minutes to 1 hour before serving.
5. Serve and Garnish:
   - Spoon the chocolate avocado mousse into dessert bowls or glasses.
   - Garnish with sliced strawberries, raspberries, chopped nuts, or shaved chocolate on top for added flavor and presentation.
6. Enjoy:
   - Serve and enjoy this delicious and nutritious Chocolate Avocado Mousse as a guilt-free dessert or snack!

This Chocolate Avocado Mousse is smooth, creamy, and full of chocolatey goodness. It's naturally sweetened with maple syrup or honey and packed with the nutritional benefits of avocados. Plus, it's quick and easy to prepare with just a few simple ingredients. Give this recipe a try for a healthier dessert option that everyone will love!

Peanut Butter Oatmeal Cookies

Ingredients:

- 1/2 cup unsalted butter, softened
- 1/2 cup creamy peanut butter
- 1/2 cup granulated sugar
- 1/2 cup packed light brown sugar
- 1 large egg
- 1 teaspoon vanilla extract
- 1 cup all-purpose flour
- 1/2 teaspoon baking soda
- 1/4 teaspoon salt
- 1 1/2 cups old-fashioned rolled oats

Optional Additions:

- 1/2 cup chocolate chips
- 1/2 cup chopped peanuts

Instructions:

1. Preheat Oven:
    - Preheat your oven to 350°F (175°C) and line baking sheets with parchment paper or silicone baking mats.
2. Cream Butter and Sugars:
    - In a large mixing bowl, cream together the softened butter, creamy peanut butter, granulated sugar, and light brown sugar until smooth and creamy.
3. Add Egg and Vanilla:
    - Beat in the egg and vanilla extract until well combined.
4. Combine Dry Ingredients:
    - In a separate bowl, whisk together the all-purpose flour, baking soda, and salt.
5. Mix Dough:
    - Gradually add the dry ingredients to the wet ingredients, mixing until just combined.
6. Add Oats (and Optional Additions):
    - Stir in the old-fashioned rolled oats until evenly distributed throughout the dough.

- Optionally, fold in chocolate chips or chopped peanuts for added flavor and texture.
7. Shape Cookies:
    - Drop tablespoon-sized portions of dough onto the prepared baking sheets, spacing them about 2 inches apart.
8. Bake Cookies:
    - Bake in the preheated oven for 10-12 minutes, or until the edges of the cookies are lightly golden brown.
    - Remove from the oven and let the cookies cool on the baking sheets for a few minutes before transferring them to wire racks to cool completely.
9. Enjoy:
    - Once cooled, serve and enjoy these delicious Peanut Butter Oatmeal Cookies with a glass of milk or your favorite beverage!

These Peanut Butter Oatmeal Cookies are soft, chewy, and packed with peanut butter flavor. The oats add a delightful texture, making them a perfect snack or dessert for any occasion. Feel free to customize the recipe with your favorite additions like chocolate chips or chopped nuts. Store any leftover cookies in an airtight container at room temperature for several days. Enjoy baking and indulging in these tasty homemade cookies!

No-Bake Pumpkin Pie

Ingredients:

For the Crust:

- 1 1/2 cups graham cracker crumbs
- 6 tablespoons unsalted butter, melted
- 2 tablespoons granulated sugar

For the Pumpkin Filling:

- 1 (15 oz) can pumpkin puree (not pumpkin pie filling)
- 1 (8 oz) package cream cheese, softened
- 1 cup powdered sugar
- 1 teaspoon vanilla extract
- 1 teaspoon ground cinnamon
- 1/2 teaspoon ground nutmeg
- 1/4 teaspoon ground cloves
- 1/4 teaspoon ground ginger
- 1/4 teaspoon salt
- 2 cups whipped cream or whipped topping (plus extra for serving, if desired)

Instructions:

1. Prepare the Crust:
    - In a mixing bowl, combine the graham cracker crumbs, melted butter, and granulated sugar. Mix until the crumbs are evenly coated.
    - Press the mixture firmly and evenly into the bottom and up the sides of a 9-inch (23cm) pie dish. Use the back of a spoon or measuring cup to pack the crust.
    - Place the crust in the refrigerator to chill while preparing the filling.
2. Make the Pumpkin Filling:
    - In a large mixing bowl, beat the softened cream cheese and powdered sugar until smooth and creamy.
    - Add the pumpkin puree, vanilla extract, ground cinnamon, nutmeg, cloves, ginger, and salt to the cream cheese mixture. Beat until well combined and smooth.
    - Gently fold in the whipped cream or whipped topping until the filling is light and fluffy.
3. Assemble the Pie:

- Spoon the pumpkin filling into the chilled graham cracker crust, spreading it out evenly with a spatula.
4. Chill and Set:
    - Cover the pie with plastic wrap and refrigerate for at least 4 hours, or preferably overnight, to allow the filling to set and flavors to meld.
5. Serve:
    - Before serving, garnish the no-bake pumpkin pie with additional whipped cream or whipped topping, if desired.
    - Slice and enjoy this delicious and creamy pumpkin pie!

This no-bake pumpkin pie is a wonderful alternative to traditional baked pies, and it's perfect for those who prefer a lighter and easier dessert option. The creamy pumpkin filling with warm spices and a buttery graham cracker crust is sure to be a hit at any fall gathering or holiday celebration. Store any leftover pie in the refrigerator. Enjoy the flavors of pumpkin spice in this delightful no-bake treat!

Almond Joy Bars

Ingredients:

For the Coconut Filling:

- 2 1/2 cups sweetened shredded coconut
- 1 (14 oz) can sweetened condensed milk
- 1 teaspoon vanilla extract

For the Chocolate Coating:

- 12 oz (about 2 cups) semi-sweet chocolate chips
- 2 tablespoons coconut oil (or vegetable oil)
- 1/2 cup whole almonds

Instructions:

1. Prepare the Coconut Filling:
    - In a mixing bowl, combine the sweetened shredded coconut, sweetened condensed milk, and vanilla extract. Mix until well combined and the mixture is sticky and holds together.
2. Form the Bars:
    - Line an 8x8-inch (20x20cm) baking dish with parchment paper or foil, leaving some overhang for easy removal later.
    - Press the coconut mixture evenly into the bottom of the prepared baking dish using a spatula or your hands. Ensure the layer is compact and smooth.
    - Place the baking dish in the refrigerator while you prepare the chocolate coating.
3. Make the Chocolate Coating:
    - In a microwave-safe bowl or using a double boiler, melt the semi-sweet chocolate chips and coconut oil together until smooth and glossy, stirring frequently to avoid burning.
    - Remove the baking dish from the refrigerator. Pour the melted chocolate mixture over the coconut layer, spreading it out evenly with a spatula.
4. Add Almonds:
    - While the chocolate is still soft, gently press whole almonds onto the surface of the chocolate layer. Space them evenly apart, as they will be cut into individual bars later.
5. Chill and Set:

- Place the baking dish back in the refrigerator for about 1-2 hours, or until the chocolate layer is completely set and firm.
6. Slice and Serve:
    - Once the Almond Joy Bars are fully set, lift them out of the baking dish using the parchment paper or foil overhang.
    - Use a sharp knife to cut the bars into desired sizes.
    - Serve and enjoy these homemade Almond Joy Bars as a delicious treat!
7. Storage:
    - Store any leftover Almond Joy Bars in an airtight container in the refrigerator for up to one week. Bring to room temperature before serving for best taste and texture.

These homemade Almond Joy Bars are perfect for satisfying your sweet cravings with a combination of coconut, chocolate, and crunchy almonds. They're great for sharing at parties, potlucks, or as a special homemade gift. Enjoy the delightful flavors of this classic candy bar in an easy-to-make and delicious dessert!

Strawberry Yogurt Pie

Ingredients:

For the Crust:

- 1 1/2 cups graham cracker crumbs
- 1/4 cup granulated sugar
- 6 tablespoons unsalted butter, melted

For the Filling:

- 1 (8 oz) package cream cheese, softened
- 1 cup plain Greek yogurt
- 1/3 cup powdered sugar
- 1 teaspoon vanilla extract
- 2 cups fresh strawberries, hulled and sliced

For the Topping:

- Additional fresh strawberries, sliced, for garnish
- Whipped cream or whipped topping, for garnish

Instructions:

1. Prepare the Crust:
    - In a mixing bowl, combine the graham cracker crumbs, granulated sugar, and melted butter. Mix until the crumbs are evenly coated.
    - Press the mixture firmly and evenly into the bottom and up the sides of a 9-inch (23cm) pie dish. Use the back of a spoon or measuring cup to pack the crust.
    - Place the crust in the refrigerator to chill while preparing the filling.
2. Make the Filling:
    - In a large mixing bowl, beat the softened cream cheese until smooth and creamy.
    - Add the Greek yogurt, powdered sugar, and vanilla extract to the cream cheese. Beat until well combined and smooth.
3. Assemble the Pie:
    - Spread half of the cream cheese and yogurt mixture into the chilled graham cracker crust, smoothing it out with a spatula.
    - Arrange half of the sliced strawberries over the filling.

- Spread the remaining cream cheese and yogurt mixture over the strawberries, covering them completely.
- Arrange the remaining sliced strawberries on top of the pie.
4. Chill and Set:
    - Cover the pie with plastic wrap or foil and refrigerate for at least 4 hours, or until the filling is set and firm.
5. Serve and Garnish:
    - Before serving, garnish the strawberry yogurt pie with additional sliced strawberries on top.
    - Optionally, add dollops of whipped cream or whipped topping around the edges of the pie for decoration.
6. Slice and Enjoy:
    - Use a sharp knife to slice the chilled pie into wedges.
    - Serve and enjoy this refreshing Strawberry Yogurt Pie as a delightful dessert!

This Strawberry Yogurt Pie is perfect for warm weather or anytime you're craving a light and fruity treat. The combination of creamy yogurt filling and fresh strawberries nestled in a graham cracker crust is sure to be a hit with family and friends. Enjoy the delicious flavors and simplicity of this no-bake dessert!

No-Bake Nutella Cheesecake

Ingredients:

For the Crust:

- 1 1/2 cups chocolate cookie crumbs (from about 20 chocolate sandwich cookies)
- 6 tablespoons unsalted butter, melted

For the Cheesecake Filling:

- 16 oz (450g) cream cheese, softened
- 1 cup Nutella (chocolate-hazelnut spread)
- 1/2 cup powdered sugar
- 1 teaspoon vanilla extract
- 1 cup heavy cream, chilled

For Garnish (optional):

- Additional Nutella, for drizzling
- Chopped hazelnuts or chocolate shavings

Instructions:

1. Prepare the Crust:
   - In a mixing bowl, combine the chocolate cookie crumbs and melted butter. Mix until the crumbs are evenly coated.
   - Press the mixture firmly and evenly into the bottom of a 9-inch (23cm) springform pan. Use the back of a spoon or measuring cup to pack the crust.
   - Place the crust in the refrigerator to chill while preparing the cheesecake filling.
2. Make the Cheesecake Filling:
   - In a large mixing bowl, beat the softened cream cheese until smooth and creamy.
   - Add the Nutella, powdered sugar, and vanilla extract to the cream cheese. Beat until well combined and smooth.
3. Whip the Heavy Cream:
   - In a separate bowl, whip the chilled heavy cream until stiff peaks form.
4. Combine and Fold:

- Gently fold the whipped cream into the Nutella cream cheese mixture until well combined and smooth.
5. Assemble the Cheesecake:
    - Spread the Nutella cheesecake filling evenly over the chilled chocolate cookie crust in the springform pan, smoothing it out with a spatula.
6. Chill and Set:
    - Cover the cheesecake with plastic wrap and refrigerate for at least 4 hours, preferably overnight, to allow the filling to set and firm up.
7. Garnish and Serve:
    - Before serving, optionally drizzle additional Nutella over the top of the cheesecake.
    - Sprinkle chopped hazelnuts or chocolate shavings on top for added decoration.
8. Slice and Enjoy:
    - Use a sharp knife to carefully remove the outer ring of the springform pan.
    - Slice the chilled Nutella cheesecake into wedges and serve.

This No-Bake Nutella Cheesecake is a crowd-pleaser and perfect for any occasion. It's rich, creamy, and bursting with chocolate-hazelnut flavor. Serve chilled and enjoy the indulgent goodness of this delightful dessert!

Lemon Coconut Truffles

Ingredients:

- 1 cup sweetened shredded coconut, plus extra for coating
- Zest of 1 lemon
- 3 tablespoons fresh lemon juice
- 1/2 cup sweetened condensed milk
- 8 oz (225g) white chocolate, finely chopped
- 1-2 drops yellow food coloring (optional, for a vibrant color)

Instructions:

1. Prepare the Coconut Mixture:
   - In a mixing bowl, combine the sweetened shredded coconut, lemon zest, lemon juice, and sweetened condensed milk. Mix until well combined.
2. Shape the Truffles:
   - Line a baking sheet with parchment paper.
   - Take small portions of the coconut mixture and roll them into balls using your hands. Place the balls on the prepared baking sheet.
   - Place the baking sheet in the refrigerator for about 30 minutes to firm up the truffles.
3. Prepare the White Chocolate Coating:
   - In a microwave-safe bowl or using a double boiler, melt the white chocolate until smooth and creamy. Stir in the yellow food coloring, if using, to achieve a lemony color.
4. Coat the Truffles:
   - Dip each chilled coconut ball into the melted white chocolate, ensuring it is fully coated. Use a fork or dipping tool to lift the truffle out of the chocolate, allowing excess chocolate to drip off.
   - Place the coated truffle back onto the parchment-lined baking sheet.
5. Decorate with Coconut:
   - Immediately sprinkle some extra sweetened shredded coconut over the wet chocolate coating of each truffle before it sets.
6. Chill and Set:
   - Place the baking sheet with the coated truffles in the refrigerator for about 15-20 minutes, or until the chocolate coating is set.
7. Serve and Enjoy:
   - Once set, transfer the lemon coconut truffles to an airtight container and store in the refrigerator until ready to serve.

- Serve chilled and enjoy these tangy, sweet, and creamy truffles as a delightful dessert or snack!

These Lemon Coconut Truffles are bursting with bright lemon flavor and the sweet taste of coconut, making them a refreshing and irresistible treat. They are perfect for sharing with family and friends or for gifting on special occasions. Enjoy making and savoring these delightful no-bake truffles!

Vegan Chocolate Mousse

Ingredients:

- 1 ripe avocado, peeled and pitted
- 1/2 cup dairy-free dark chocolate chips or chopped chocolate (ensure it's vegan)
- 1/4 cup unsweetened cocoa powder
- 1/4 cup maple syrup or agave nectar
- 1 teaspoon vanilla extract
- Pinch of salt
- 1/4 cup coconut cream (from a can of full-fat coconut milk, chilled)

Optional Garnish:

- Fresh berries
- Shredded coconut
- Vegan whipped cream

Instructions:

1. Melt the Chocolate:
    - In a microwave-safe bowl or using a double boiler, melt the dairy-free dark chocolate until smooth. Stir frequently to prevent burning. Let it cool slightly.
2. Blend Ingredients:
    - In a food processor or blender, combine the ripe avocado, melted chocolate, unsweetened cocoa powder, maple syrup or agave nectar, vanilla extract, and a pinch of salt.
    - Blend until smooth and creamy, scraping down the sides as needed to ensure everything is well combined.
3. Add Coconut Cream:
    - Open a can of full-fat coconut milk that has been chilled in the refrigerator overnight. Scoop out the solid coconut cream that has separated at the top (reserve the liquid for another use).
    - Add the coconut cream to the chocolate avocado mixture in the blender or food processor.
    - Blend again until everything is smooth and incorporated. The coconut cream helps to add richness and creaminess to the mousse.
4. Chill the Mousse:
    - Transfer the vegan chocolate mousse to serving dishes or small jars.

    - Cover and refrigerate for at least 2 hours, or until the mousse is chilled and set.
5. Serve and Garnish:
    - Before serving, garnish the vegan chocolate mousse with fresh berries, shredded coconut, or a dollop of vegan whipped cream if desired.
6. Enjoy:
    - Serve and enjoy this deliciously creamy Vegan Chocolate Mousse as a satisfying dessert or sweet treat!

This Vegan Chocolate Mousse is smooth, rich, and perfect for chocolate lovers looking for a dairy-free and egg-free dessert option. The avocado provides a creamy texture while the dark chocolate and cocoa powder give it a deep, indulgent flavor. Try making this mousse for a special occasion or anytime you're craving a decadent chocolate dessert that's plant-based and delicious!

No-Bake Caramel Apple Cheesecake Bars

Ingredients:

For the Crust:

- 2 cups graham cracker crumbs
- 1/2 cup unsalted butter, melted
- 2 tablespoons granulated sugar

For the Cheesecake Filling:

- 16 oz (450g) cream cheese, softened
- 1/2 cup powdered sugar
- 1 teaspoon vanilla extract
- 1 cup whipped cream or whipped topping

For the Apple Topping:

- 2 large apples, peeled, cored, and diced (use a sweet variety like Honeycrisp or Gala)
- 2 tablespoons unsalted butter
- 1/4 cup packed light brown sugar
- 1/2 teaspoon ground cinnamon
- Pinch of salt

For the Caramel Drizzle:

- 1/2 cup store-bought or homemade caramel sauce

Instructions:

1. Prepare the Crust:
    - In a mixing bowl, combine the graham cracker crumbs, melted butter, and granulated sugar. Mix until the crumbs are evenly coated.
    - Press the mixture firmly and evenly into the bottom of a 9x13-inch (23x33cm) baking dish lined with parchment paper. Use the back of a spoon or measuring cup to pack the crust.
    - Place the crust in the refrigerator to chill while preparing the cheesecake filling and apple topping.
2. Make the Cheesecake Filling:
    - In a large mixing bowl, beat the softened cream cheese until smooth and creamy.

- Add the powdered sugar and vanilla extract to the cream cheese. Beat until well combined.
- Gently fold in the whipped cream or whipped topping until the filling is light and fluffy.
3. Spread the Cheesecake Filling Over the Crust:
    - Remove the chilled crust from the refrigerator.
    - Spread the prepared cheesecake filling evenly over the chilled crust in the baking dish. Use a spatula to smooth out the surface.
4. Prepare the Apple Topping:
    - In a skillet or saucepan, melt the unsalted butter over medium heat.
    - Add the diced apples, brown sugar, ground cinnamon, and a pinch of salt to the skillet.
    - Cook the apples, stirring occasionally, until they are tender and caramelized (about 5-7 minutes).
    - Remove from heat and let the apple mixture cool slightly.
5. Top the Cheesecake Bars with Apple Mixture:
    - Spoon the cooked apple mixture evenly over the cheesecake filling layer in the baking dish.
6. Chill and Set:
    - Place the baking dish in the refrigerator for at least 2 hours, or until the cheesecake bars are chilled and set.
7. Drizzle with Caramel Sauce:
    - Before serving, drizzle the caramel sauce over the top of the chilled cheesecake bars.
8. Slice and Serve:
    - Use a sharp knife to cut the chilled caramel apple cheesecake bars into squares.
    - Serve and enjoy these delicious no-bake bars as a decadent dessert!

These No-Bake Caramel Apple Cheesecake Bars are perfect for fall or any time of year when you're craving a sweet and creamy treat. The combination of creamy cheesecake, caramelized apples, and buttery graham cracker crust is simply irresistible. Try making these bars for your next gathering or special occasion!

No-Bake Pistachio Cream Pie

Ingredients:

For the Crust:

- 1 1/2 cups graham cracker crumbs
- 6 tablespoons unsalted butter, melted
- 2 tablespoons granulated sugar

For the Pistachio Cream Filling:

- 1 (3.4 oz) package instant pistachio pudding mix
- 1 3/4 cups cold milk
- 8 oz (1 package) cream cheese, softened
- 1/2 cup powdered sugar
- 1 teaspoon vanilla extract
- 1 cup heavy cream, chilled

For Garnish (optional):

- Chopped pistachios
- Whipped cream

Instructions:

1. Prepare the Crust:
   - In a mixing bowl, combine the graham cracker crumbs, melted butter, and granulated sugar. Mix until the crumbs are evenly coated.
   - Press the mixture firmly and evenly into the bottom and up the sides of a 9-inch (23cm) pie dish. Use the back of a spoon or measuring cup to pack the crust.
   - Place the crust in the refrigerator to chill while preparing the filling.
2. Make the Pistachio Cream Filling:
   - In a large mixing bowl, whisk together the instant pistachio pudding mix and cold milk until smooth. Set aside.
3. Prepare the Cream Cheese Mixture:
   - In another mixing bowl, beat the softened cream cheese, powdered sugar, and vanilla extract until smooth and creamy.
4. Combine and Whip:
   - Gradually add the prepared pistachio pudding mixture to the cream cheese mixture, beating until well combined and smooth.

5. Whip the Heavy Cream:
   - In a separate bowl, whip the chilled heavy cream until stiff peaks form.
6. Fold and Assemble:
   - Gently fold the whipped cream into the pistachio cream cheese mixture until smooth and incorporated.
7. Fill the Pie Crust:
   - Pour the pistachio cream filling into the chilled graham cracker crust, spreading it out evenly with a spatula.
8. Chill and Set:
   - Cover the pie with plastic wrap and refrigerate for at least 4 hours, preferably overnight, to allow the filling to set and firm up.
9. Garnish and Serve:
   - Before serving, garnish the chilled pistachio cream pie with chopped pistachios and a dollop of whipped cream, if desired.
10. Slice and Enjoy:
    - Use a sharp knife to cut the chilled pistachio cream pie into slices.
    - Serve and enjoy this creamy and flavorful no-bake dessert!

This No-Bake Pistachio Cream Pie is a delicious and refreshing dessert that's perfect for pistachio lovers. The creamy filling with a hint of nutty pistachio flavor, combined with the buttery graham cracker crust, makes it a delightful treat for any occasion. Make this pie for family gatherings, potlucks, or special celebrations, and watch it disappear with smiles all around!

Raspberry Chia Pudding

Ingredients:

- 1 cup fresh raspberries (or frozen and thawed)
- 2 tablespoons maple syrup or honey
- 1 teaspoon vanilla extract
- 1/4 cup chia seeds
- 1 cup coconut milk (or any plant-based milk of choice)
- Optional toppings: additional raspberries, sliced almonds, shredded coconut

Instructions:

1. Prepare the Raspberry Puree:
    - In a blender or food processor, puree the fresh raspberries until smooth.
    - If desired, strain the raspberry puree through a fine mesh sieve to remove seeds. This step is optional if you prefer a smoother texture.
2. Sweeten the Raspberry Puree:
    - Transfer the raspberry puree to a bowl and stir in the maple syrup (or honey) and vanilla extract. Adjust sweetness to taste.
3. Combine Chia Seeds and Raspberry Mixture:
    - Add the chia seeds to the raspberry mixture and stir well to combine.
    - Let the mixture sit for about 5-10 minutes, stirring occasionally to prevent clumping.
4. Add Coconut Milk:
    - Gradually pour in the coconut milk while stirring the chia seed mixture. Continue stirring until well combined.
5. Chill and Set:
    - Cover the bowl with plastic wrap or transfer the mixture into individual serving jars or bowls.
    - Refrigerate for at least 2-3 hours, or preferably overnight, to allow the chia seeds to absorb the liquid and thicken into a pudding-like consistency.
6. Serve and Enjoy:
    - Once chilled and set, give the Raspberry Chia Pudding a good stir.
    - Divide the pudding into serving dishes and top with additional fresh raspberries, sliced almonds, or shredded coconut if desired.
7. Variations:
    - Feel free to experiment with different fruits like strawberries, blueberries, or blackberries for variations of this chia pudding.

- You can also adjust the sweetness by using more or less maple syrup (or honey) according to your preference.

Raspberry Chia Pudding is a nutritious and satisfying dessert that's loaded with fiber, omega-3 fatty acids from chia seeds, and antioxidants from fresh raspberries. It's dairy-free, gluten-free, and can be enjoyed as a healthy breakfast, snack, or dessert. Make a batch of this delicious pudding and enjoy its refreshing flavor and creamy texture!

No-Bake S'mores Bars

Ingredients:

- 3 cups mini marshmallows
- 4 1/2 cups crispy rice cereal (like Rice Krispies)
- 1/2 cup unsalted butter
- 1/2 cup packed light brown sugar
- 1 teaspoon vanilla extract
- 1/4 teaspoon salt
- 1 1/2 cups milk chocolate chips
- 1 cup graham cracker crumbs

Instructions:

1. Prepare the Pan:
    - Line a 9x13-inch baking dish with parchment paper or aluminum foil, leaving an overhang on the sides for easy removal later. Lightly grease with cooking spray.
2. Melt Marshmallows and Butter:
    - In a large microwave-safe bowl, combine the mini marshmallows and butter. Microwave in 30-second intervals, stirring in between, until the marshmallows and butter are melted and smooth.
3. Add Flavorings:
    - Stir in the light brown sugar, vanilla extract, and salt until well combined.
4. Combine with Cereal:
    - Add the crispy rice cereal to the marshmallow mixture and gently fold until the cereal is evenly coated.
5. Press into Pan:
    - Transfer half of the cereal mixture into the prepared baking dish. Use a greased spatula or your hands to press the mixture firmly and evenly into the bottom of the pan.
6. Sprinkle with Chocolate Chips and Graham Cracker Crumbs:
    - Sprinkle half of the milk chocolate chips and half of the graham cracker crumbs evenly over the pressed cereal mixture in the pan.
7. Layer Remaining Cereal Mixture:
    - Spread the remaining cereal mixture over the chocolate and graham cracker layer. Press down firmly to create an even surface.
8. Add Toppings:

- Sprinkle the remaining milk chocolate chips and graham cracker crumbs over the top of the bars, pressing them lightly into the cereal mixture.
9. Chill and Set:
    - Refrigerate the bars for at least 1-2 hours, or until firm and set.
10. Slice and Serve:
    - Use the parchment paper or foil overhang to lift the bars out of the baking dish. Transfer to a cutting board and slice into squares.
11. Enjoy:
    - Serve and enjoy these delicious No-Bake S'mores Bars as a fun and tasty treat!

These No-Bake S'mores Bars are perfect for summer gatherings, picnics, or whenever you're craving the classic s'mores flavor in a convenient bar form. They're gooey, crunchy, and full of chocolatey, marshmallow goodness. Store any leftovers in an airtight container at room temperature for up to several days. Enjoy making and sharing these delightful bars with family and friends!

Chocolate Covered Strawberry Truffles

Ingredients:

- 1 cup fresh strawberries, hulled and chopped
- 8 oz (225g) semi-sweet or dark chocolate, finely chopped
- 1/3 cup heavy cream
- 1 tablespoon unsalted butter, softened
- 1 teaspoon vanilla extract
- Pinch of salt
- 8 oz (225g) milk or dark chocolate, for coating

Optional Garnish:

- White chocolate, melted (for drizzling)
- Sprinkles or edible decorations

Instructions:

1. Prepare the Strawberry Ganache:
    - Place the chopped strawberries in a blender or food processor and blend until smooth.
    - In a saucepan, combine the strawberry puree, heavy cream, butter, vanilla extract, and salt over medium heat. Stir continuously until the mixture is heated through and starts to simmer.
2. Melt the Chocolate:
    - Place the finely chopped semi-sweet or dark chocolate in a heatproof bowl.
    - Pour the hot strawberry cream mixture over the chopped chocolate. Let it sit for 1-2 minutes to soften the chocolate.
    - Stir the mixture until smooth and well combined. This is your strawberry ganache. If any chocolate pieces remain unmelted, you can microwave the mixture in short bursts (10-15 seconds) and stir until smooth.
3. Chill the Ganache:
    - Transfer the strawberry ganache to a shallow dish or bowl. Cover with plastic wrap, ensuring the plastic wrap touches the surface of the ganache to prevent a skin from forming.
    - Refrigerate the ganache for at least 2-3 hours, or until firm enough to scoop and roll into balls.
4. Shape the Truffles:

- Once the ganache is firm, use a small spoon or melon baller to scoop out portions of the ganache.
- Roll each portion between your palms to form smooth balls. Place the rolled truffles on a parchment-lined baking sheet.
- Refrigerate the truffles for another 15-20 minutes to firm up.

5. Coat with Chocolate:
   - Melt the milk or dark chocolate for coating in a heatproof bowl set over a pot of simmering water (double boiler method) or in the microwave, stirring frequently until smooth.
   - Using a fork or dipping tool, dip each chilled strawberry truffle into the melted chocolate, coating it completely. Allow any excess chocolate to drip back into the bowl.

6. Optional Garnish:
   - Place the dipped truffles back onto the parchment-lined baking sheet. If desired, drizzle melted white chocolate over the truffles or sprinkle with decorative toppings before the chocolate sets.

7. Chill and Serve:
   - Refrigerate the chocolate covered strawberry truffles until the chocolate coating is set, about 30 minutes to 1 hour.
   - Serve and enjoy these delightful homemade truffles as a special treat!

These Chocolate Covered Strawberry Truffles are a delightful combination of fruity sweetness and rich chocolate, making them a perfect treat for chocolate lovers and strawberry enthusiasts alike. Store any leftover truffles in an airtight container in the refrigerator for up to one week. Enjoy making and savoring these elegant truffles!

No-Bake Berry Icebox Cake

Ingredients:

- 1 pound (450g) fresh berries (strawberries, blueberries, raspberries, blackberries)
- 2 cups heavy cream, chilled
- 1/2 cup powdered sugar
- 1 teaspoon vanilla extract
- 1 package (about 9 ounces) of your favorite cookies (like graham crackers, vanilla wafers, or ladyfingers)
- Fresh mint leaves, for garnish (optional)

Instructions:

1. Prepare the Berries:
    - Wash and dry the berries. If using strawberries, hull and slice them into thin slices. Set aside.
2. Make the Whipped Cream:
    - In a large mixing bowl, combine the chilled heavy cream, powdered sugar, and vanilla extract.
    - Use an electric mixer or whisk to beat the cream until stiff peaks form. Be careful not to over-whip.
3. Assemble the Icebox Cake:
    - Spread a thin layer of whipped cream on the bottom of a serving dish or 9x13-inch baking dish to create a base.
    - Arrange a layer of cookies over the whipped cream, covering the bottom of the dish. You may need to break some cookies to fit them into corners.
    - Spread a layer of whipped cream over the cookies, covering them completely.
    - Arrange a layer of mixed berries over the whipped cream.
4. Repeat Layers:
    - Repeat the layering process: cookies, whipped cream, and berries, until you reach the top of the dish or run out of ingredients. The final layer should be a generous topping of whipped cream and berries.
5. Chill the Icebox Cake:
    - Cover the dish with plastic wrap and refrigerate the icebox cake for at least 4 hours, or overnight, to allow the flavors to meld and the cookies to soften into a cake-like texture.
6. Serve:

- Before serving, garnish the top of the icebox cake with additional fresh berries and mint leaves, if desired.
- Slice and serve this delicious No-Bake Berry Icebox Cake chilled.
7. Enjoy:
    - Enjoy the creamy, fruity goodness of this refreshing dessert with family and friends!

This No-Bake Berry Icebox Cake is a perfect dessert for summer gatherings or anytime you want a cool and satisfying treat. Feel free to customize the cake with your favorite berries and cookies for endless flavor combinations. Make this delightful icebox cake ahead of time and wow your guests with its beautiful presentation and delicious taste!

Mango Lime Sorbet

Ingredients:

- 3 ripe mangoes, peeled, pitted, and diced (about 4 cups of diced mango)
- Zest and juice of 2 limes
- 1/2 cup granulated sugar, or to taste
- 1/2 cup water
- Optional: Fresh mint leaves, for garnish

Instructions:

1. Prepare the Mangoes:
    - Peel the ripe mangoes and remove the pits. Dice the mango flesh into chunks.
2. Make the Simple Syrup:
    - In a small saucepan, combine the granulated sugar and water. Heat over medium heat, stirring occasionally, until the sugar is completely dissolved. Remove from heat and let the simple syrup cool to room temperature.
3. Blend the Sorbet Base:
    - In a blender or food processor, combine the diced mangoes, lime zest, lime juice, and cooled simple syrup.
    - Blend until smooth and creamy. Taste the mixture and adjust sweetness by adding more sugar if needed, depending on the sweetness of your mangoes.
4. Chill the Mixture:
    - Transfer the blended mango-lime mixture to a bowl or container. Cover and refrigerate for at least 1-2 hours to chill thoroughly.
5. Churn in an Ice Cream Maker (Optional):
    - If you have an ice cream maker, pour the chilled mango-lime mixture into the machine and churn according to the manufacturer's instructions until it reaches a soft-serve consistency.
6. Freeze the Sorbet:
    - Transfer the churned or unchurned mango-lime mixture into a shallow, freezer-safe container.
    - Cover the container with plastic wrap or a lid to prevent ice crystals from forming on the surface.
    - Place the sorbet in the freezer and let it freeze for at least 4-6 hours, or until firm.
7. Serve and Garnish:

- When ready to serve, use a scoop to portion the Mango Lime Sorbet into bowls or glasses.
- Garnish with fresh mint leaves for an extra pop of color and flavor, if desired.
8. Enjoy:
    - Serve and enjoy this refreshing Mango Lime Sorbet as a delightful dessert or palate cleanser between courses.

This Mango Lime Sorbet is dairy-free, vegan-friendly, and bursting with tropical flavors. It's a healthy and refreshing dessert option that's easy to make at home. Experiment with different citrus fruits or add a splash of rum for a grown-up twist. Enjoy this cool and tangy treat on a hot day or anytime you're craving a taste of the tropics!

No-Bake Cinnamon Rolls

Ingredients:

For the "Dough":

- 2 cups almond flour
- 1/4 cup coconut oil, melted
- 1/4 cup maple syrup or honey
- 1 teaspoon vanilla extract
- Pinch of salt

For the Cinnamon Filling:

- 1/4 cup coconut oil, softened
- 1/4 cup maple syrup or honey
- 2 tablespoons ground cinnamon

For the Icing:

- 1/2 cup powdered sugar
- 1-2 tablespoons almond milk or any milk of choice
- 1/2 teaspoon vanilla extract

Instructions:

1. Prepare the "Dough" Mixture:
    - In a mixing bowl, combine the almond flour, melted coconut oil, maple syrup (or honey), vanilla extract, and a pinch of salt. Mix until a dough-like consistency forms. If the mixture is too dry, add a little more melted coconut oil.
2. Roll Out the Dough:
    - Place the dough mixture between two sheets of parchment paper.
    - Use a rolling pin to roll out the dough into a rectangle, about 1/4-inch thick.
3. Make the Cinnamon Filling:
    - In a small bowl, mix together the softened coconut oil, maple syrup (or honey), and ground cinnamon to create the filling.
4. Spread the Filling:
    - Remove the top layer of parchment paper from the rolled-out dough.
    - Spread the cinnamon filling evenly over the dough, leaving a small border around the edges.
5. Roll Up the Dough:

- Starting from one long side, carefully roll up the dough into a tight log.
- Use the parchment paper to help lift and roll the dough.
- Once rolled, place the log in the refrigerator to chill for about 1 hour, or until firm.

6. Slice the Rolls:
   - Remove the chilled dough log from the refrigerator.
   - Use a sharp knife to slice the log into individual rolls, about 1-inch thick.
7. Prepare the Icing:
   - In a small bowl, whisk together the powdered sugar, almond milk (or milk of choice), and vanilla extract until smooth and creamy. Adjust the consistency by adding more milk if needed.
8. Serve:
   - Drizzle the prepared icing over the chilled cinnamon rolls.
   - Enjoy your no-bake cinnamon rolls immediately!

These No-Bake Cinnamon Rolls are a quick and delicious treat that captures the classic flavors of cinnamon rolls without the need for baking. They're perfect for a sweet breakfast, snack, or dessert. Store any leftovers in the refrigerator for up to a few days. Simply warm them slightly before serving for a gooey and delightful treat!

Blueberry Lemon Cheesecake Bars

Ingredients:

For the Crust:

- 1 1/2 cups graham cracker crumbs
- 1/4 cup granulated sugar
- 1/2 cup unsalted butter, melted

For the Cheesecake Filling:

- 16 oz (450g) cream cheese, softened
- 1/2 cup granulated sugar
- 2 large eggs
- Zest and juice of 1 lemon
- 1 teaspoon vanilla extract

For the Blueberry Topping:

- 1 1/2 cups fresh or frozen blueberries
- 1/4 cup granulated sugar
- 1 tablespoon cornstarch
- Zest and juice of 1 lemon

Instructions:

1. Preheat the Oven:
    - Preheat your oven to 350°F (175°C). Grease or line a 9x9-inch (23x23cm) baking pan with parchment paper, leaving an overhang for easy removal.
2. Make the Crust:
    - In a mixing bowl, combine the graham cracker crumbs, granulated sugar, and melted butter. Mix until well combined.
    - Press the mixture evenly into the bottom of the prepared baking pan. Use the back of a spoon or a flat-bottomed glass to compact the crust.
3. Bake the Crust:
    - Bake the crust in the preheated oven for 8-10 minutes, or until lightly golden. Remove from the oven and set aside.
4. Prepare the Cheesecake Filling:
    - In a large mixing bowl, beat the softened cream cheese and granulated sugar until smooth and creamy.

- Add the eggs, lemon zest, lemon juice, and vanilla extract. Beat until well combined and smooth.
5. Pour and Bake:
    - Pour the cheesecake filling over the baked crust, spreading it out evenly with a spatula.
6. Make the Blueberry Topping:
    - In a small saucepan, combine the blueberries, granulated sugar, cornstarch, lemon zest, and lemon juice.
    - Cook over medium heat, stirring frequently, until the mixture thickens and the blueberries burst slightly, about 5-7 minutes.
    - Remove from heat and let the blueberry mixture cool slightly.
7. Add Blueberry Topping:
    - Spoon the slightly cooled blueberry mixture over the cheesecake layer, spreading it out evenly.
8. Bake and Cool:
    - Return the pan to the oven and bake for an additional 25-30 minutes, or until the cheesecake is set and the edges are lightly golden.
    - Remove from the oven and let the cheesecake bars cool completely in the pan on a wire rack.
9. Chill and Serve:
    - Once cooled to room temperature, transfer the pan to the refrigerator and chill the cheesecake bars for at least 2-3 hours, or until firm.
10. Slice and Enjoy:
    - Use the parchment paper overhang to lift the chilled cheesecake bars out of the pan.
    - Cut into squares and serve these delicious Blueberry Lemon Cheesecake Bars chilled.

These Blueberry Lemon Cheesecake Bars are perfect for summer gatherings, potlucks, or any occasion where you want to impress with a fruity and creamy dessert. The combination of lemony cheesecake and sweet blueberries is simply irresistible! Store any leftovers in the refrigerator for up to several days. Enjoy making and savoring these delightful bars!

Pistachio Coconut Squares

Ingredients:

For the Base:

- 1 cup all-purpose flour
- 1/2 cup unsalted butter, softened
- 1/4 cup granulated sugar

For the Filling:

- 1 cup sweetened shredded coconut
- 1 cup shelled pistachios, finely chopped
- 1 can (14 oz) sweetened condensed milk
- 1 teaspoon vanilla extract
- 1/4 teaspoon salt

For Topping (optional):

- 1/2 cup white chocolate chips or chopped white chocolate
- 1 teaspoon coconut oil (for melting chocolate)

Instructions:

1. Preheat the Oven:
    - Preheat your oven to 350°F (175°C). Grease or line an 8x8-inch (20x20cm) baking dish with parchment paper, leaving an overhang for easy removal.
2. Make the Base:
    - In a mixing bowl, combine the softened butter, flour, and granulated sugar. Use a fork or pastry cutter to mix until crumbly and well combined.
    - Press the mixture evenly into the bottom of the prepared baking dish.
3. Bake the Base:
    - Bake the base in the preheated oven for 15-18 minutes, or until lightly golden. Remove from the oven and let it cool slightly.
4. Prepare the Filling:
    - In a separate mixing bowl, combine the shredded coconut, chopped pistachios, sweetened condensed milk, vanilla extract, and salt. Mix until well combined.
5. Assemble and Bake:
    - Spread the coconut-pistachio filling evenly over the slightly cooled base in the baking dish.

- Return the dish to the oven and bake for an additional 20-25 minutes, or until the edges are golden brown and the filling is set.
6. Cool and Add Topping (optional):
    - Allow the pistachio coconut squares to cool completely in the baking dish on a wire rack.
    - If desired, melt the white chocolate chips with coconut oil in the microwave or over a double boiler until smooth. Drizzle the melted chocolate over the cooled squares.
7. Chill and Serve:
    - Refrigerate the baking dish for at least 1-2 hours, or until the squares are chilled and firm.
    - Use the parchment paper overhang to lift the chilled squares out of the baking dish. Cut into squares and serve.

These Pistachio Coconut Squares are a delightful blend of nutty pistachios, sweet coconut, and a buttery base. They make a perfect treat for parties, gatherings, or as a sweet indulgence for yourself. Store any leftovers in an airtight container in the refrigerator for several days. Enjoy these delicious and easy-to-make squares!

No-Bake Almond Butter Cookies

Ingredients:

- 1 cup creamy almond butter (or any nut butter of choice)
- 1/2 cup honey or maple syrup
- 1/2 cup coconut oil, melted
- 2 teaspoons vanilla extract
- 3 cups old-fashioned oats (gluten-free if needed)
- 1/2 cup unsweetened shredded coconut (optional)
- Pinch of salt (if using unsalted almond butter)

Instructions:

1. Mix Wet Ingredients:
    - In a large mixing bowl, combine the creamy almond butter, honey (or maple syrup), melted coconut oil, and vanilla extract. Stir until smooth and well combined.
2. Add Dry Ingredients:
    - Add the old-fashioned oats, unsweetened shredded coconut (if using), and a pinch of salt (if using unsalted almond butter) to the wet mixture. Stir until all ingredients are fully incorporated and the mixture holds together.
3. Shape Cookies:
    - Line a baking sheet with parchment paper.
    - Scoop about 1-2 tablespoons of the cookie mixture and roll it into a ball using your hands.
    - Place the formed cookie balls onto the prepared baking sheet, spacing them apart.
4. Chill and Set:
    - Once all the cookies are shaped, place the baking sheet in the refrigerator for about 30 minutes, or until the cookies firm up and hold their shape.
5. Serve and Enjoy:
    - Remove the chilled almond butter cookies from the refrigerator.
    - Store any leftover cookies in an airtight container in the refrigerator for up to a week.

These No-Bake Almond Butter Cookies are a wholesome and delicious treat that's perfect for a quick snack or dessert. They are naturally sweetened and can be customized with your favorite add-ins like chocolate chips, dried fruit, or nuts. Enjoy making and savoring these easy and healthy cookies!

Chocolate Cherry Icebox Cake

Ingredients:

- 2 cups heavy cream, chilled
- 1/2 cup powdered sugar
- 1 teaspoon vanilla extract
- 2 packages (about 9 ounces each) chocolate wafer cookies
- 1 can (21 ounces) cherry pie filling
- Chocolate shavings or cocoa powder, for garnish (optional)

Instructions:

1. Prepare the Whipped Cream:
    - In a large mixing bowl, combine the chilled heavy cream, powdered sugar, and vanilla extract.
    - Use an electric mixer or whisk to beat the cream until stiff peaks form. Set aside.
2. Assemble the Icebox Cake:
    - Spread a thin layer of whipped cream on the bottom of a 9x13-inch (23x33cm) baking dish or serving dish.
    - Arrange a layer of chocolate wafer cookies over the whipped cream, covering the bottom of the dish.
3. Add Cherry Filling:
    - Spoon about half of the cherry pie filling over the layer of cookies, spreading it out evenly.
4. Layer Whipped Cream:
    - Spread a layer of whipped cream over the cherry filling, covering it completely.
5. Repeat Layers:
    - Continue layering with another layer of chocolate wafer cookies, remaining cherry pie filling, and more whipped cream until you've used up all the ingredients.
    - Finish with a final layer of whipped cream on top.
6. Chill the Cake:
    - Cover the dish with plastic wrap and refrigerate the icebox cake for at least 4 hours, or preferably overnight, to allow the flavors to meld and the cookies to soften.
7. Serve and Garnish:

- Before serving, garnish the chilled icebox cake with chocolate shavings or a dusting of cocoa powder, if desired.
8. Slice and Enjoy:
    - Use a sharp knife to slice the chilled Chocolate Cherry Icebox Cake into squares.
    - Serve and enjoy this delicious and creamy no-bake dessert!

This Chocolate Cherry Icebox Cake is perfect for summer gatherings, potlucks, or any occasion where you want to impress with a decadent yet easy-to-make dessert. The combination of chocolate, cherries, and whipped cream is simply irresistible. Store any leftovers in the refrigerator for a few days. Enjoy making and savoring this delightful icebox cake!

Lemon Coconut Energy Bites

Ingredients:

- 1 cup Medjool dates, pitted (about 10-12 dates)
- 1 cup unsweetened shredded coconut, plus extra for rolling
- Zest of 1 lemon
- Juice of 1 lemon
- 1/2 teaspoon vanilla extract
- Pinch of salt

Instructions:

1. Prepare Dates:
    - If your dates are not already pitted, remove the pits. Then, soak the dates in warm water for 10-15 minutes to soften them.
2. Combine Ingredients:
    - In a food processor, combine the soaked and drained dates, shredded coconut, lemon zest, lemon juice, vanilla extract, and a pinch of salt.
    - Process the mixture until it forms a sticky dough-like consistency. The mixture should easily hold together when pressed.
3. Form into Balls:
    - Scoop out tablespoon-sized portions of the mixture and roll them between your hands to form smooth balls.
    - If the mixture is too sticky to handle, wet your hands slightly with water.
4. Roll in Coconut:
    - Roll each ball in additional shredded coconut to coat them evenly. This adds extra flavor and texture.
5. Chill and Serve:
    - Place the lemon coconut energy bites on a plate or baking sheet lined with parchment paper.
    - Chill the energy bites in the refrigerator for at least 30 minutes to firm up.
6. Enjoy:
    - Once chilled, your Lemon Coconut Energy Bites are ready to enjoy!
    - Store any leftover energy bites in an airtight container in the refrigerator for up to a week.

These Lemon Coconut Energy Bites are perfect for snacking on-the-go, providing a boost of energy from the natural sugars in dates and the refreshing flavor of lemon.

They are also vegan, gluten-free, and refined sugar-free. Make a batch of these tasty bites and keep them handy for whenever you need a quick and healthy treat!

No-Bake Cappuccino Pie

Ingredients:

For the Crust:

- 1 1/2 cups chocolate sandwich cookie crumbs (about 20 cookies)
- 6 tablespoons unsalted butter, melted

For the Filling:

- 1 tablespoon instant coffee granules or espresso powder
- 1 tablespoon hot water
- 8 oz (225g) cream cheese, softened
- 1/2 cup powdered sugar
- 1 teaspoon vanilla extract
- 1 cup heavy cream, chilled
- 1/2 cup semi-sweet chocolate chips, melted and cooled slightly
- Chocolate shavings or cocoa powder, for garnish (optional)

Instructions:

1. Prepare the Crust:
    - In a mixing bowl, combine the chocolate cookie crumbs and melted butter. Stir until the crumbs are evenly coated with butter.
2. Press into Pie Dish:
    - Press the crumb mixture firmly and evenly into the bottom and up the sides of a 9-inch (23cm) pie dish or tart pan. Use the back of a spoon or a flat-bottomed glass to press the crumbs down.
3. Prepare the Coffee Mixture:
    - In a small bowl, dissolve the instant coffee granules or espresso powder in hot water. Set aside to cool slightly.
4. Make the Filling:
    - In a large mixing bowl, beat the softened cream cheese, powdered sugar, and vanilla extract until smooth and creamy.
5. Add Coffee and Chocolate:
    - Add the dissolved coffee mixture to the cream cheese mixture and beat until well combined.
    - Gradually add the chilled heavy cream to the mixture and continue beating until stiff peaks form.
    - Fold in the melted semi-sweet chocolate chips until evenly incorporated.

6. Fill the Crust:
    - Spoon the cappuccino filling into the prepared chocolate crust, spreading it out evenly with a spatula.
7. Chill the Pie:
    - Cover the pie with plastic wrap and refrigerate for at least 4 hours, or until the filling is set and firm.
8. Garnish and Serve:
    - Before serving, garnish the chilled cappuccino pie with chocolate shavings or a dusting of cocoa powder, if desired.
9. Slice and Enjoy:
    - Slice the pie into wedges and serve chilled.

This No-Bake Cappuccino Pie is a delightful dessert that's perfect for any occasion, from casual gatherings to special dinners. It's creamy, rich, and full of coffee and chocolate flavor. Make this easy and impressive pie to satisfy your sweet cravings with a touch of caffeine! Store any leftover pie in the refrigerator for up to several days. Enjoy making and savoring this delicious cappuccino pie!

Strawberry Pretzel Salad Bars

Ingredients:

For the Pretzel Crust:

- 2 cups crushed pretzels
- 3/4 cup unsalted butter, melted
- 3 tablespoons granulated sugar

For the Cream Cheese Filling:

- 8 oz (225g) cream cheese, softened
- 1 cup powdered sugar
- 1 teaspoon vanilla extract
- 1 cup whipped topping (such as Cool Whip)

For the Strawberry Layer:

- 3 cups sliced fresh strawberries
- 1 cup boiling water
- 1 package (3 oz) strawberry gelatin (such as Jell-O)

Instructions:

1. Preheat the Oven:
    - Preheat your oven to 350°F (175°C). Grease or line a 9x13-inch (23x33cm) baking dish with parchment paper.
2. Make the Pretzel Crust:
    - In a mixing bowl, combine the crushed pretzels, melted butter, and granulated sugar.
    - Press the mixture firmly and evenly into the bottom of the prepared baking dish.
    - Bake the crust in the preheated oven for 10 minutes. Remove from the oven and let it cool completely.
3. Prepare the Cream Cheese Filling:
    - In another mixing bowl, beat the softened cream cheese, powdered sugar, and vanilla extract until smooth and creamy.
    - Fold in the whipped topping until well combined.
    - Spread the cream cheese filling over the cooled pretzel crust. Ensure the filling reaches the edges of the crust to create a seal.
4. Prepare the Strawberry Layer:

- Place the sliced strawberries evenly over the cream cheese filling.
- In a heatproof bowl, dissolve the strawberry gelatin in boiling water, stirring until completely dissolved.
- Let the strawberry gelatin mixture cool slightly, then pour it gently and evenly over the strawberries.

5. Chill the Bars:
    - Refrigerate the bars for at least 2-3 hours, or until the gelatin layer is set and firm.
6. Slice and Serve:
    - Once fully chilled and set, use a sharp knife to slice the Strawberry Pretzel Salad Bars into squares.
    - Serve and enjoy these delightful and refreshing bars!

These Strawberry Pretzel Salad Bars are a perfect dessert for picnics, potlucks, or any occasion where you want a sweet and satisfying treat. The combination of crunchy pretzel crust, creamy filling, and juicy strawberries with a hint of gelatin is simply irresistible. Store any leftover bars in the refrigerator for up to several days. Enjoy making and savoring these delicious strawberry pretzel bars!

Pineapple Coconut Tarts

Ingredients:

For the Tart Shells:

- 1 1/2 cups all-purpose flour
- 1/4 cup granulated sugar
- 1/2 cup unsalted butter, cold and cut into small pieces
- 1 large egg yolk
- 2-3 tablespoons cold water

For the Pineapple Coconut Filling:

- 1 can (20 oz) crushed pineapple, drained well
- 1 cup sweetened shredded coconut
- 1/2 cup granulated sugar
- 2 tablespoons cornstarch
- 1/4 teaspoon salt
- 1 teaspoon vanilla extract

Optional Topping:

- Whipped cream or vanilla ice cream, for serving
- Additional shredded coconut, toasted (for garnish)

Instructions:

1. Make the Tart Shells:
    - In a food processor, combine the flour and granulated sugar. Add the cold butter pieces and pulse until the mixture resembles coarse crumbs.
    - Add the egg yolk and 2 tablespoons of cold water. Pulse again until the dough begins to clump together. If needed, add another tablespoon of water, a little at a time, until the dough forms.
    - Turn the dough out onto a lightly floured surface and gather it into a ball. Flatten into a disc, wrap in plastic wrap, and refrigerate for at least 30 minutes.
2. Preheat the Oven:
    - Preheat your oven to 375°F (190°C). Lightly grease a muffin tin with butter or cooking spray.
3. Prepare the Filling:

- In a mixing bowl, combine the drained crushed pineapple, sweetened shredded coconut, granulated sugar, cornstarch, salt, and vanilla extract. Mix well until everything is combined.
4. Assemble the Tarts:
    - On a lightly floured surface, roll out the chilled dough to about 1/8-inch thickness. Use a round cookie cutter or glass that is slightly larger than the muffin tin cavities to cut out circles of dough.
    - Press each dough circle gently into the prepared muffin tin cavities, shaping them into tart shells.
5. Fill the Tart Shells:
    - Spoon the pineapple coconut filling evenly into each tart shell, filling them almost to the top.
6. Bake the Tarts:
    - Place the muffin tin in the preheated oven and bake for 20-25 minutes, or until the tart shells are golden brown and the filling is bubbly.
7. Cool and Serve:
    - Allow the Pineapple Coconut Tarts to cool in the muffin tin for a few minutes, then carefully remove them and transfer to a wire rack to cool completely.
    - Serve the tarts warm or at room temperature, optionally topped with whipped cream or a scoop of vanilla ice cream.
    - Garnish with toasted shredded coconut, if desired.
8. Enjoy:
    - Enjoy these delicious Pineapple Coconut Tarts as a delightful dessert or snack!

These Pineapple Coconut Tarts are sure to be a hit with their tropical flavors and buttery tart shells. They can be enjoyed warm or at room temperature, and they make a lovely addition to any dessert table or afternoon tea. Store any leftover tarts in an airtight container at room temperature for up to a few days. Enjoy making and savoring these delightful treats!

No-Bake Maple Walnut Cheesecake

Ingredients:

For the Crust:

- 1 1/2 cups graham cracker crumbs
- 1/2 cup walnuts, finely chopped
- 1/4 cup unsalted butter, melted
- 2 tablespoons maple syrup

For the Cheesecake Filling:

- 16 oz (450g) cream cheese, softened
- 1/2 cup powdered sugar
- 1 cup heavy cream, chilled
- 1/4 cup maple syrup
- 1 teaspoon vanilla extract
- 1/2 cup chopped walnuts, for topping

Instructions:

1. Prepare the Crust:
    - In a mixing bowl, combine the graham cracker crumbs, finely chopped walnuts, melted butter, and maple syrup. Mix until well combined and the mixture resembles wet sand.
2. Press into Pan:
    - Press the crust mixture evenly into the bottom of a 9-inch (23cm) springform pan or pie dish. Use the back of a spoon or a flat-bottomed glass to compact the crust. Place the pan in the refrigerator to chill while you prepare the filling.
3. Make the Cheesecake Filling:
    - In a large mixing bowl, beat the softened cream cheese and powdered sugar until smooth and creamy.
    - In a separate bowl, whip the chilled heavy cream until stiff peaks form.
    - Gently fold the whipped cream into the cream cheese mixture.
    - Add the maple syrup and vanilla extract, and mix until smooth and well combined.
4. Assemble the Cheesecake:
    - Remove the chilled crust from the refrigerator.

- Pour the cheesecake filling over the crust, spreading it out evenly with a spatula.
5. Chill the Cheesecake:
    - Cover the cheesecake with plastic wrap and refrigerate for at least 4 hours, or until firm and set.
6. Top with Walnuts:
    - Before serving, sprinkle the chopped walnuts evenly over the chilled cheesecake.
7. Slice and Serve:
    - Use a sharp knife to slice the No-Bake Maple Walnut Cheesecake into wedges or squares.
    - Serve chilled and enjoy!

This No-Bake Maple Walnut Cheesecake is creamy, decadent, and full of wonderful maple and walnut flavors. It's a perfect dessert for special occasions or gatherings, and it's sure to impress your family and friends. Store any leftover cheesecake covered in the refrigerator for up to a few days. Enjoy making and savoring this delightful dessert!

Vegan Chocolate Peanut Butter Pie

Ingredients:

For the Crust:

- 1 1/2 cups crushed vegan chocolate sandwich cookies (about 20 cookies)
- 1/4 cup melted coconut oil
- Pinch of salt

For the Peanut Butter Filling:

- 1 cup creamy peanut butter
- 1/2 cup pure maple syrup or agave nectar
- 1/4 cup melted coconut oil
- 1 teaspoon vanilla extract
- Pinch of salt

For the Chocolate Ganache Topping:

- 1/2 cup dairy-free chocolate chips
- 1/4 cup full-fat coconut milk

Optional Toppings:

- Chopped peanuts
- Vegan whipped cream or coconut whipped cream

Instructions:

1. Prepare the Crust:
    - In a mixing bowl, combine the crushed chocolate cookies, melted coconut oil, and a pinch of salt. Mix until well combined.
    - Press the mixture firmly into the bottom and up the sides of a 9-inch (23cm) pie dish to form the crust. Place it in the refrigerator to set while you prepare the filling.
2. Make the Peanut Butter Filling:
    - In a microwave-safe bowl or small saucepan, melt the coconut oil.
    - In a mixing bowl, whisk together the creamy peanut butter, pure maple syrup (or agave nectar), melted coconut oil, vanilla extract, and a pinch of salt until smooth and creamy.
3. Fill the Crust:
    - Remove the prepared crust from the refrigerator.

- Pour the peanut butter filling into the crust and spread it out evenly with a spatula.
4. Prepare the Chocolate Ganache Topping:
    - In a microwave-safe bowl or small saucepan, heat the coconut milk until it starts to simmer.
    - Pour the hot coconut milk over the dairy-free chocolate chips and let it sit for 1-2 minutes.
    - Stir until smooth and well combined to make the chocolate ganache.
5. Top the Pie:
    - Pour the chocolate ganache over the peanut butter filling in the pie crust, spreading it out evenly.
6. Chill and Set:
    - Place the pie in the refrigerator to chill for at least 4 hours, or until firm and set.
7. Serve and Enjoy:
    - Once the pie is chilled and set, garnish with chopped peanuts and vegan whipped cream or coconut whipped cream, if desired.
    - Slice and serve this delicious Vegan Chocolate Peanut Butter Pie!

This Vegan Chocolate Peanut Butter Pie is a decadent and indulgent dessert that's perfect for special occasions or any time you're craving a sweet treat. It's creamy, rich, and full of irresistible chocolate and peanut butter flavors. Store any leftover pie covered in the refrigerator for up to several days. Enjoy making and savoring this delightful vegan dessert!

Matcha Green Tea Coconut Bars

Ingredients:

For the Matcha Coconut Base:

- 1 1/2 cups shredded coconut (unsweetened)
- 1/2 cup almond flour or oat flour
- 1/4 cup coconut oil, melted
- 1/4 cup maple syrup or agave nectar
- 1 tablespoon matcha green tea powder
- 1 teaspoon vanilla extract
- Pinch of salt

For the Matcha Coconut Layer:

- 1 1/2 cups shredded coconut (unsweetened)
- 1/4 cup coconut butter, softened
- 2 tablespoons coconut oil, melted
- 2 tablespoons maple syrup or agave nectar
- 1 tablespoon matcha green tea powder
- 1 teaspoon vanilla extract
- Pinch of salt

Instructions:

1. Prepare the Matcha Coconut Base:
    - In a food processor, combine the shredded coconut and almond flour (or oat flour). Pulse until the mixture becomes finely ground.
    - Add the melted coconut oil, maple syrup (or agave nectar), matcha green tea powder, vanilla extract, and a pinch of salt. Process until well combined and sticky.
    - Press the mixture firmly and evenly into the bottom of an 8x8-inch (20x20cm) baking dish lined with parchment paper. Place it in the freezer while you prepare the next layer.
2. Make the Matcha Coconut Layer:
    - In the food processor (no need to clean it), combine the shredded coconut, softened coconut butter, melted coconut oil, maple syrup (or agave nectar), matcha green tea powder, vanilla extract, and a pinch of salt.
    - Process until well combined and the mixture starts to come together.

- Remove the baking dish from the freezer and spread the matcha coconut layer evenly over the base layer.
3. Chill and Set:
    - Place the baking dish back in the freezer for at least 1-2 hours, or until the bars are firm and set.
4. Slice and Serve:
    - Once the Matcha Green Tea Coconut Bars are fully chilled and set, lift them out of the baking dish using the parchment paper.
    - Use a sharp knife to slice the bars into squares or rectangles.
    - Serve and enjoy these delightful matcha coconut bars! Store any leftovers in an airtight container in the refrigerator or freezer.

These Matcha Green Tea Coconut Bars are perfect for green tea lovers looking for a unique and healthy dessert. They're refreshing, flavorful, and packed with nutritious ingredients. Make a batch of these bars to enjoy as a snack or dessert throughout the week. Enjoy making and savoring these delightful matcha treats!

No-Bake Red Velvet Cake

Ingredients:

For the Cake Layers:

- 2 1/2 cups crushed chocolate sandwich cookies (such as Oreos), cream filling removed (about 25 cookies)
- 1/2 cup melted butter

For the Cream Cheese Filling:

- 16 oz (450g) cream cheese, softened
- 1 cup powdered sugar
- 1 teaspoon vanilla extract
- 1 cup heavy cream, chilled

For Assembly and Decoration:

- 1 tablespoon unsweetened cocoa powder
- Red food coloring (gel or liquid), as needed
- White chocolate curls or sprinkles (optional)

Instructions:

1. Prepare the Cake Layers:
    - In a food processor, pulse the chocolate sandwich cookies until finely crushed.
    - Add the melted butter to the crushed cookies and pulse until the mixture resembles wet sand.
    - Press the cookie mixture firmly and evenly into the bottom of a 9-inch (23cm) springform pan to form the first cake layer. Place in the refrigerator to set while you prepare the filling.
2. Make the Cream Cheese Filling:
    - In a large mixing bowl, beat the softened cream cheese, powdered sugar, and vanilla extract until smooth and creamy.
    - In a separate bowl, whip the chilled heavy cream until stiff peaks form.
    - Gently fold the whipped cream into the cream cheese mixture until well combined.
3. Add Red Velvet Flavor:

- Add the unsweetened cocoa powder and red food coloring to the cream cheese filling, adjusting the amount of food coloring until you achieve the desired shade of red and the flavor resembles red velvet cake. Mix well.

4. Assemble the Cake:
   - Remove the springform pan from the refrigerator.
   - Spread half of the red velvet cream cheese filling over the chilled cookie crust, smoothing it out with a spatula.
   - Place another layer of crushed chocolate sandwich cookies over the cream cheese filling to create the second cake layer.
   - Spread the remaining red velvet cream cheese filling over the cookie layer, smoothing it out evenly.

5. Chill and Decorate:
   - Cover the cake with plastic wrap and refrigerate for at least 4 hours, or until the filling is set and firm.
   - Before serving, decorate the top of the cake with white chocolate curls or sprinkles for a festive touch.

6. Slice and Serve:
   - Carefully release the cake from the springform pan.
   - Use a sharp knife to slice the No-Bake Red Velvet Cake into wedges.
   - Serve chilled and enjoy this delightful no-bake dessert!

This No-Bake Red Velvet Cake is a creative and simplified version of the classic cake, perfect for occasions when you want to enjoy the flavors of red velvet without turning on the oven. It's creamy, decadent, and sure to impress your guests. Store any leftovers in the refrigerator for up to several days. Enjoy making and savoring this delicious no-bake treat!

www.ingramcontent.com/pod-product-compliance
Lightning Source LLC
LaVergne TN
LVHW081601060526
838201LV00054B/2002